Building a Leadership Pipeline

for

Deans in Business Schools

Dr. Wolfgang Amann

wp walnutpublication
.com

INDIA • UK • USA

Paperback ISBN: 978-1-954399-60-0

Hardback ISBN: 978-1-954399-61-7

eBook ISBN: 978-1-954399-62-4

First Published in February 2021

Published by Walnut Publication (an imprint of Vyusta Ventures LLP)

www.walnutpublication.com

USA

6834 Cantrell Road #2096, Little Rock, AR 72207, USA

India

#722, Esplanade One, Rasulgarh, Bhubaneswar – 751010, India

#55 S/F, Panchkuian Marg, Connaught Place, New Delhi - 110001, India

UK

International House, 12 Constance Street, London E16 2DQ, United Kingdom

Acknowledgements

I express my gratitude to all study participants. These deans and interviewees have an especially packed agenda. I am thankful for their availability. Several experts in the field supported this project as well. I want to acknowledge the tremendous efforts done by Dr. Rita Kop, Dr. Anne Qualter, Dr. Peter Kahn and Dr. Seng Kok. Their feedback on earlier drafts help evolve the thinking and the research presented in this book. Finally, I am grateful for the final editing carried out by Wilhelm Retief and Amelia Burger as part of Ilse Evertse & Associates.

Wolfgang Amann, 1 February 2021

Contents

List of figures

List of tables

1. Introduction

1.1. The personal interest in the topic

When it comes to sound leadership of organisations, "the fish rot starts from its head" (Rothstein, 2013, p. 1009), implying that without sound leadership at the top, the rest of the organisation faces challenges in order to perform well. Insufficiencies at the upper echelon would cascade down and penetrate the entire organisation.

Having worked in business schools for more than two decades, this insight intuitively applies to business schools and also features in my observations. I have personally experienced the extreme ends of a continuum ranging from a business school that is almost perfectly led on one end to a perpetual crises-prone business school at the other. A school that I joined for a few years was legally organised as a non-profit. It was so successful that, in order to avoid profits every few years, the school either added a building or tore one down to replace it with a fancier one. The school paid the staff well, the staff was engaged and well trained. The faculty support functions were cutting edge and so were the human resources (HR) and information technology (IT) practices. Faculty created innovative teaching cases and thought leadership books in their field. Turnover was low and innovation as well as thought leadership initiatives prospered.

I have similarly experienced the other end of the continuum with an institution that had an average staff tenure of only two years. Building an effective organisational culture and strong routines as well as securing knowledge and experience were close to impossible. Several staff members experienced verbal abuse. Several of them were in tears after experiencing these verbal attacks. The dean frequently shouted at colleagues, pretending to know each and every task better than the hired specialist. An atmosphere of fear and ambiguity instead of clear responsibility and accountability prevailed. Under the reign of a micromanaging, inexperienced dean, research and innovation came to a standstill. The quality of programmes suffered. This institution withdrew approved budgets without reasons and did the same with granted leave applications for vacation, messing up long-planned family holidays. Two years into his tenure, the dean had a nervous breakdown and wept in front of his colleagues at a staff meeting. He was burned out. His reputation was equally burnt, as complaints disqualified him for future leadership roles in the school. By then, many of the best talents had already left the organisation.

At another organisation I experienced, the law enforcement authorities arrested the school's president temporarily, following allegations of him channelling public funds into his private accounts. He was acquitted completely. When it comes to charismatic leadership, out-of-the-box thinking and effective organizational strategizing, he showed a remarkable brilliance and clearly stood out. Yet, the school's reputation, student numbers and, linked to them, the overall financial performance suffered so drastically that a competitor could take over the once highly prestigious elite school (cf. Schwertfeger, 2019a, 2019b). Power games could not have gotten any worse. It seems that it really gets lonely at the top.

I have personally experienced the good, the bad and the ugly. These experiences triggered my interest for this research project, as I was convinced that the situation of sound business school leadership was not a fatalistic one. Having experienced better and worse places myself sparked my interest in the upper echelon of business schools and, more precisely, in the question: How should business school deans prepare themselves for their responsibilities?

Linked to this question are several sub-questions, such as: What is truly the function of a business school dean? What challenges do they face? Are these challenges manageable and if so, how? Teaching business courses on leadership and governance, I was aware of the leadership pipeline concept in the corporate sector (Singer, 2014). Individuals go through various stages and transitions – if they choose to do so and if their organisations notice their potential for performance. Yet, how can aspiring individuals interested in leading a business school prepare themselves for their future assignments? Would a leadership pipeline for business schools work? Does it have to be an idiosyncratic leadership pipeline or would the corporate world version suffice?

Since the perception is that many business schools are not very differentiated due to an ongoing McDonaldisation process (Amann, 2017), challenges and true adversity appear most important for deans. Iñiguez de Onzoño and Carmona (2012) add the concept and label of the Red Queen effect to the analysis of management formation and business schools. In evolutionary theory and biology, the Red Queen effect prescribes everlasting change and adaptation for mere survival. According to this effect within the business-school context, they ought to embrace constant and never-ending change to merely stay in the game and thus survive.

Kambil and Budnik (2013) view taking the reins at a business school as the hardest thing and Davies (2016), for example, even asks whether business school deans are doomed, as there is so much adversity to cope with. In light of these challenges and limited resources, D'Alessio and Avolio (2011) asked somewhat cynically whether we need deans or rather magicians to handle the situation. Demands on institutions always appear to outpace, at least to a certain extent, the institution's ability to deliver, leaving management education as a field awash with fulfilled and unfulfilled promises (Thomas et al., 2013).

The discussions on the further development of business schools are often not constructive enough. Many scholars attack business schools with harsh criticism, for example, for being hijacked by the elites (Spender & Locke, 2011) or for being unable to convey proper values, which turn them into "silent partners in crime" (Swanson & Frederick, 2011, p. 24). Therefore, I aim to adopt a more constructive approach, pathing the route to a solution. If there were effective leadership pipelines in place at business schools, a generation of deans, well equipped to cope with the adversity, could mature over time.

In addition to improving practice, this research project also aims to help reflect on individual career paths. As for myself, I had leadership roles when establishing a law school, a supply chain school, a university, an academy, and serve on a number of university boards or help steer education initiatives. In addition, I have been working on the concept of HUBS – humanistic business schools – for more than a decades, leading to a number of books, keynote speeches and underlying research projects. It is crucial to regularly reflect not only about what institutions we want but if we have the right skills to build and sustain them. It is my intent to provide such reflection opportunities for you as the reader.

There is an obvious gap in the literature, as, for example, Davies (2015) reviews the growing demands on deans and concludes her study clarifying "the business school leadership pipeline needs to be supported" (p. 3). Yet, real research into this leadership pipeline is, by and large, missing.

Since I was keen to learn from more sources than my employer, the corresponding research, setting out to further explore the phenomenon of the leadership pipeline of business schools, had to be broader, more international and diverse to capture ideas and solutions, which is why interviews took place throughout Europe, the Middle East, and North Africa (MENA) region. The following section provides an overview of the analysis.

1.2. Structure of the analysis

Overall, this book follows the ambition to develop a theory truly grounded in data, thus applying a grounded theory approach. Therefore, Chapter 2 continues with a preliminary literature overview in line with constructivist grounded theory, which sees value in gaining an understanding of selected sensitising concepts. This can then help with the fieldwork and coding process (Charmaz, 2014). The above-mentioned overview produces an initial critical review of the literature, i.e. what is already known about the topic and what the crucial gaps are.

Chapter 3 takes the research further by detailing how this research question, – of how business school deans perceive the leadership-development phenomenon, – is addressed. The underlying assumptions, options and choices are presented. Details on how data were analysed ensue – along with a critical evaluation of the chosen methodology and method.

Chapter 4 presents and discusses the empirical results. The constructed categories and overall new grounded theory explore and help understand the phenomenon under scrutiny better. The theory is linked to and is discussed within the context of additional literature. Chapter 5 follows the logic of Borton (1970), who maintains that holistic problem-solving requires answers to three key questions: "what"', addressing what the problem really is; next is "so what?" – the inquiry into the gained insight's true meaning; and lastly, "now what?" – the future-oriented curiosity about what should be done. In other words, chapter 5, after initially summarising limitations, outlines implications for theory and practice. As for the recommendations for practice, they aim at two groups: Firstly, current deans will gain an opportunity to reflect on how their learning journey developed in the light of gained insights and how they could improve practices in their institutions. Secondly, aspiring next-generation leaders in business schools can gain crucial insights into becoming a dean and proactively preparing for it. Chapter 6 revisits the research objectives and presents final conclusions on gained insights.

2. Preliminary literature review

2.1. Introduction to the logic of the literature review in a grounded-theory-based study

According to Fink (2005), a literature review is systematic and suitably broad in scope with a clear approach. It is explicit in how and why it was carried out and comprehensive in relying on all relevant material to become reproducible for others. Rousseau et al. (2008) add that a literature review ought to include a reflective interpretation of the relevant literature. This section, thus, aims to create this transparency regarding the ensuing literature review's purpose and structure. The literature's logic spans a classic requisite variety view (Ashby, 2011) on the topic. The concept prescribes that an organisation mirrors internally the complexity it faces externally, such that effective coping can occur as visualised in the following figure.

Figure 1: A requisite variety logic for the literature review

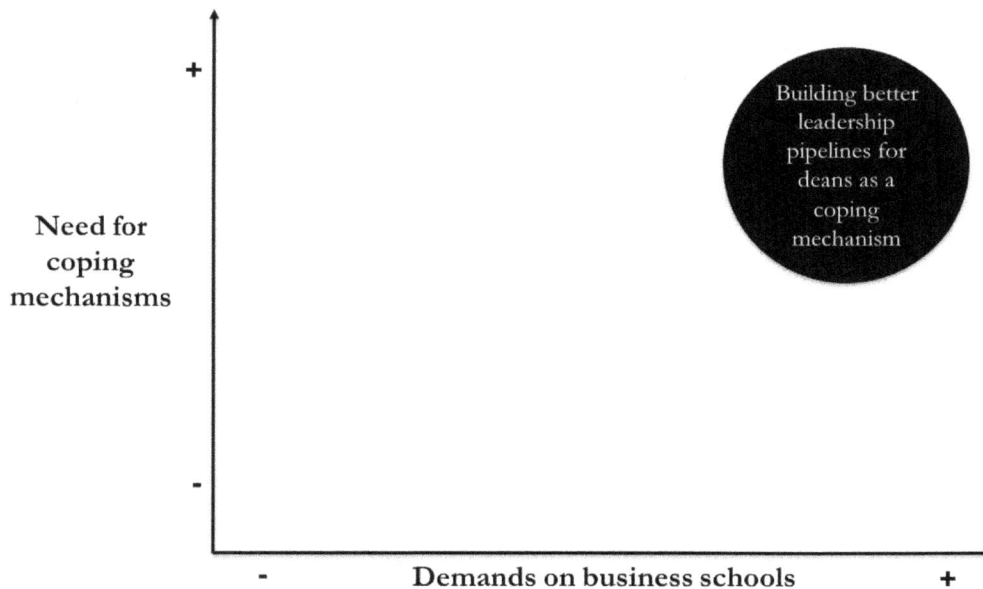

Section 2.2 critically reviews these challenges in management education and adds a preliminary analysis of implications for the dean role. Section 2.3 focuses on the business school as the main institution and once again elaborates on implications for the dean role. As the figure above suggests, building leadership pipelines for business schools could be a possible coping mechanism. Therefore, section

2.4 defines and reviews the role of deans while presenting an overview of expected traits. Sections 2.5 and 2.6 deal with leadership and leadership pipelines, including considerations for deans from this more general view. Section 2.7 provides a critical evaluation of this preliminary literature review and summarises the research gaps.

Purpose of the literature review in a grounded-theory-based study

Before embarking on these sections, it is necessary to clarify the overall purpose of and the link to the subsequent research methodology chapter as well as the overall research process. As indicated and as Chapter 3 details further, this research project relies on a grounded theory approach. This has repercussions on the very role of the literature review. According to Glaser (2001) as one of the founders of grounded theory, reviewing the literature can actually cause more harm than benefit, since it might tempt the researcher to rather search for data fitting extant literature and available theories, which stifles innovation. Scott (2009) argues similarly by encouraging researchers to be more open to emerging concepts in how they identify them based on their perception.

Others disagree. Charmaz (2006), for example, rejects this view of a researcher's limited capabilities and posits that the literature review can inform without running the risk of prejudices in the form of premature judgments. This self-sensitisation towards relevant concepts can facilitate a more reflexive researcher's coding process (Charmaz, 2014). Since literature on leadership pipelines in the corporate sector exists, awareness of particular transitions can help sensitise towards learning and unlearning needs. As this research project relies on constructivist grounded theory, it embraces the benefits of selected sensitising concepts (see further detail on the research methodology in Chapter 3).

The following section starts this preliminary literature review by clarifying just how major the demands on business schools are as outlined in the literature. Changes are fundamental and even if an institution found solutions, critical events like COVID-19 can render identified solutions outdated or less effective.

2.2. Challenges in management education and resulting demands for leadership and leadership development in business schools

The literature review for this section was carried out in a similar manner as for the subsequent sections. I followed a systematic approach proposed by Wohlin (2014). He suggested that the literature should initially be screened in a forward and backward snowballing. Initially, keywords were created, such as "challenges in business schools" or "changes in business schools". I entered the keywords in academic databases via the University of Liverpool's library and into Google Scholar via https://scholar.google.com/, which follows a different search engine algorithm. "Backward snowballing" (Wohlin, 2014, p. 3) encouraged me to scrutinise the bibliography and individual articles listed at the end of publications. I gave preference to peer-reviewed articles published more recently, as industry trends could change over time. Abstracts were screened first. If these articles contained key words or concepts, a process of forward snowballing started in which I re-entered these new keywords, such as "MOOCs", into the search engines.

Thereafter, a process of repeated divergence and convergence ensued. Divergence expanded the search for more and different articles and topics. Convergence explored how to best integrate and condense ongoing debates and themes. The following section presents the result of the final convergence. Reviewing the growing literature on management education in general and business schools in particular (based on the approach of backward and forward snowballing), shows that the following key developments challenge business schools and their leaders. Three main topic clusters in the form of mega-challenges emerge in this phase of a sensitising literature review: 1) more external orientation, 2) teaching and learning innovations and 3) implementing holistic internal change. As portrayed in the following and to anticipate the result, these trends create adversity – and business schools must ensure that they have the right leaders in place to cope with the challenges. These three clusters lead to growing demands on the dean role.

Mega-challenge 1: Increasing external orientation and overcoming the valley of death

The increasing external orientation is a top trend in business education (Nikitina & Lapina, 2017). Moreover, Lorange (2002) outlines how business schools become more market orientated, rethinking the value that they create. According to Mintzberg (2004), a management as well as a management education expert, institutions were criticised for only producing Master of Business Administration (MBA) degree graduates, not true managers. Others argued similarly and represent voices that started to be heard. Many have repeatedly questioned the relevance of business schools, which appear to have developed in the wrong direction (Bennis & O'Toole, 2005).

A number of authors outline drivers of this derailing. According to Buttler (2008), studies by the Ford Foundation and the Carnegie Foundation in 1959 caused a tremendous gap to appear between rigorous research on one side and practical relevance on the other. Both publications criticised research as insufficiently rigorous, calling for the integration of approaches and tools from natural sciences. De Frutos-Belizon, Martin-Alcazar and Sanchez-Gardey (2017) label this gap the valley of death, which persists and has been a theme in numerous top journals, such as the Academy of Management Journal (2001), the British Journal of Management (2001), Human Resources Management (2004), the Journal of Management Studies (2009), Organization Studies (2010), the Academy of Management Perspectives (2012) and the Journal of Business Economics (2014). Generally, stakeholder demands increase – beyond corporations. Very recently, Tourish (2020) argues that an even more severe perversion of the trend towards irrelevance emerges. He argues that people start writing articles not even contemplating the goal to enhance theory but to rather advance careers. Based on wrong motivations and a lack of something to say, Tourish identifies the rise of imposters in business schools as part of a triumph-of-nonsense movement.

Business schools are under fire (Amann et al., 2011) from various sides. The financial crisis, which haunted organisations after 2007, caused scrutiny of business school graduates' insufficient ethical background, although new content was also proposed (Forray et al., 2015). Swanson and Frederick (2011) even label institutions "silent partners in corporate crime" (p. 24). Over the last years, all key international accreditations have integrated sustainability as another course evaluation criterion (Nicholls et al., 2013). Beyond accreditations, the United Nations' Global Compact Principles of Responsible Management Education (PRME) initiative (Wersun, 2017) and the Sustainable Development Goals (SDGs) have increased their expectations from business schools and business school leaders (Storey et al., 2017). Accredited business schools and PRME signatory institutions must report regularly on progress.

This call for more ethics, relevance and practice orientation may not be as easy to fulfil as it appears. Seybolt (1996) argues in favour of protecting the business school's technical core, which is its research, as sometimes asking unpopular questions or taking more time or pursuing more conceptual innovations still add value, although the research cycle of closing with practical implications must be fostered. Paton et al. (2014) equally argue in favour of more plurality of ideas being developed even if they initially diverge from mainstream practical thinking. How to grow a business school's strength, – for example, in fundraising or teaching, – without neutralising another strength, – for example, in research or career services, – therefore represents a challenge for the upper echelon in business schools. A clear and unique vision and mission ought to be considered and an overall alignment should be ensured.

Meta-challenge 2: Revamping of teaching and learning

Besides the content dimensions, overall andragogic innovations challenge established organisational solutions. Nikitina and Lapina (2017) view teaching methods as becoming substantially more flexible. Technological change generally disrupts both classic teaching methods and business models, for example, through massive open online courses (MOOCs) providing content with very different scale and cost effects (Burd et al., 2015). With sufficient quality-level videos on basically all core business topics being available for free at Khan Academy and the likes, as well as on youtube.com, basic knowledge and skills training have become a commodity. In this context, Datar et al. (2010) clarify that the knowledge level of learning is the easiest and that the other levels need to be emphasized more than in the past.

Nikitina and Lapina as well as Datar et al. maintain that besides knowing the models, facts and figures, "the doing" has become increasingly important as a learning goal and outcome. Can graduates apply the lessons learnt? Can they carry out organisational improvements effectively? Furthermore, the "being level" has grown in importance. Have students reflected critically on the question of the kind of leaders they aspire to be? Together, these questions form the essential pedagogical pillars.

By creating this enhanced, more multi-dimensional value, third parties can hold business schools even more accountable than before. Good schools pursue and maintain international accreditations and comply proactively with external third-party evaluations (Durand & Dameron, 2017). Their value creation can no longer be internal black boxes but should be transparent and reported on. In executive education, business schools as suppliers need to deliver measurable outcomes.

As far back as 1976, Kirkpatrick (1976) suggested moving towards a more differentiated model of learning levels, namely a learner's initial reaction to a learning intervention in the form of course satisfaction surveys, gained knowledge, perceived behavioural change and perceived value in the form of relevance to employers. Philips (1996) suggested measuring the return on investment more directly. Institutions are encouraged to produce and report on more tangible outcomes that will pass scrutiny tests, and accreditation hurdles. This is the key challenge for business schools and deans.

Mega-challenge 3: Holistic internal change

Successful organisational evolution and the driving home of results are additional challenges. Brandenburg and Federkeil (2007) note that while business schools have also made major progress in terms of internationalisation, it challenges established structures and budgets (Altbach & Knight, 2007). Internationalisation initiatives often do not achieve the expected outcomes, as performance tends to be more volatile or even deteriorate during the different stages of foreign expansion (Contractor, Kumar, & Kundu, 2007). According to Ghemawat (2007), more adversity is yet to come, because the world has not even achieved semi-globalisation. Consequently, Wladimir (2017) warns that organisational leaders should expect internationalisation and globalisation to result in even more complexity.

Furthermore, sources of business school funding, especially from governments and even corporations paying for tuitions, have changed fundamentally in many countries, requiring more entrepreneurship (Estermann et al., 2013). Current business models erode and business schools search for new revenues (Durand & Dameron, 2017). Nikitina and Lapina (2017) report that institutions currently partner or build clusters and networks to create more value.

Resulting demands for leadership and leadership development in business schools

Regardless of whether a business school faces the core challenges of the need to listen more to and comply with external stakeholder demands or to organise for learning innovations and holistic organisational change, business school leaders and their institutions need to ready themselves for the challenges and adversity ahead. These trends have far-reaching consequences and require business schools, rather like the corporate sector, to encourage transformational leaders in order to ensure the business schools' survival and evolution (Landsberg, 2003).

Pfeffer (2009) supports this train of thought, acknowledging that sound leadership development matters as much in higher education as in companies. In line with Hewitt's (2009) insight that great companies have good leaders, business schools should also benefit from sound leadership development and promotion. Bolden, Petrov, Gosling and Bryman (2009) confirm and express this more strongly, viewing deans as being at the heart of organisational transformation. This view – labelled the great man theory in the literature – has, however, come under increasing attack, since the actual antecedents that moderate and mediate these, as well as more secondary, contextual factors, impact organisational performance in more complex manners. Nonetheless, a business school leader can have an important and identifiable impact. Reviewing the literature on leadership development in higher education, Hassan (2013) concludes that while research on leadership in the industry and the corporate world is substantial, there is a true paucity of research in the higher education context in general and business schools in particular.

Applying the logic of Ashby's (2011) requisite variety, it is necessary to assess the aforementioned challenges of internationalisation, technological changes, changing sources of funding and shifting stakeholder demands relatively – relative to the degree to which organisations, including business schools, have internally built the complexity and capabilities to cope with adversity. How to create business school leaders who are skilled and versatile enough to adequately cope with the adversity that the trends outlined above generate, remains rather unclear. This question, therefore, reveals a research gap. Most of the research related to leadership development in business schools has focused on the participants in these institutions' programmes, but not on the business schools' leadership development needs (cf., e.g., Pfeffer, 2009).

My research project deals with an idea that could and should spill over from the corporate sector into business schools more than it has to date. The corporate sector has relied on advanced insights and models on how to create leadership pipelines (Charan et al., 2011). These pipelines outline how talents move through different career stages. In the research project at hand, these pipelines are the core concept that will be explored for importation into the higher education sector in general and business schools in particular.

There is as yet no such leadership pipeline concept for business schools, which the literature review in the following will show. Before delving into the literature, the following section sheds light on the diversity of business schools. This heterogeneity entails different job profiles for and demand levels on deans.

2.3. Types of business schools and implications of institutional needs for the dean role

Business schools are diverse (Lorange, 2008). D'Alessio and Avolio (2011) go as far as stating that "there is no single model or size for business schools" (p. 21). Even in the US, which has a long-standing MBA culture, there are, according to Engwall (2007), many variations that are likely to create differences amongst the paths that institutions embark on when internationalising.

One can find the first explanation for this variation in the historical developments. According to Thomas et al. (2013), four countries, i.e. France, Germany, the UK and the US, have been driving the success of management education as a field since the 19th century – with "business schools" being the US term for these institutions aspiring to educate the practising manager. One can distinguish five generations of institutions (cf. Fragueiro & Thomas, 2011, and Thomas & Wilson, 2011).

- The 19th and early 20th century and, thus, the first generation institutions were trade schools in a vocational era. They had a strong national focus, determining their size.

- The subsequent period or second generation schools up to the 1970s continued this national orientation of schools, yet with the US model becoming a stronger reference point.

- Third generation schools in the period from the 1970s to the 1990s experienced even more dominance of the US business school logic with national lead institutions having set clear reputational structures and brand identities. Simultaneously, international benchmarking and competition, for example, in rankings or for membership in accreditation bodies emerged, forcing institutions to explore strategic moves, such as alliances and intensified foreign activities.

- Fourth generation institutions from 1990 to 2005 experienced a reaction to the rising criticism of the US business school logic. A more dominant European identity and less mimicry of US schools followed. A case in point is the spread of one-year MBA programmes in Europe versus a two-year track in the US. The Bologna process fostered pan-European mobility and a homogenisation of the higher education system (Wihlborg & Robson, 2019). Simultaneously, competition in the field of rigorous research characterised schools on both sides of the Atlantic.

- Fifth generation schools post-2005 experienced more emphasis on globalisation, especially a move beyond Western, i.e. Northern hemisphere, thinking to include Eastern business philosophies and markets. With both the Western and Eastern business philosophies peaking ever since, the attention has been more on sustainability in the classroom and teaching efforts, moving further away from the idea that Milton increasingly views as dated, i.e. that "the business of business is business" (Lai et al., 2017) only.

The above-mentioned overview of the generations and the evolution of business schools clarify that business schools have come a long way since what Simon (1991) referred to as "a wasteland of vocationalism" (p. 139). The brief history of business schools explains, to a certain extent, the diversity encountered internationally, for example, their age and organisational identity versus their international reach over time as well.

Another means of characterising the diversity of business schools can stem from their overall orientation. Davies and Hilton (2014) argue that business schools inevitably have to specialise and concentrate their resources. Ivory, Misekll, Shipton, White and Moeslein (2006) outline a framework for positioning institutions in their report on the future of business schools in the UK.

The authors identify two core dimensions and distinguish between institutions strongly focused on scholarly impact versus organisational impact and their commitment towards teaching versus research. This results in a four-quadrant matrix distinguishing four types of institutions as portrayed in the following figure. It describes the organisational focus, primary stakeholders, key performance indicators (KPI) and prioritised investments.

A knowledge economy aims at contributing research activities to organisational impact. In turn, a professional school targets organisational impact via teaching. A social science set-up prefers to pursue scholarly impact with thorough research activities and, lastly, a liberal arts set-up promotes scholarly impact through teaching. The authors detail exactly how diverging the practices of recruitment and retention, dissemination and impact as well as reputation might be in these institutions; thus, the key success factors for institutions and, therefore, the demands on leadership require different positioning.

Next to explaining the diversity of business schools historically or by mapping their orientation, Lorange (2012) differentiates between various types of business schools: the adaptive business school, the proactive business school, the entrepreneurial business school, the rationally managed business school and the dynamic business school. Each main type challenges the institution's leadership differently. The adaptive school merely reacts and, thus, – unlike a proactive school, – does not have to rely on the best thought leaders in research or teaching.

An entrepreneurial institution with noteworthy bottom-up initiatives requires a different organisational culture, talent and budget management when juxtaposed to a rationally and, thus, often more centrally and hierarchically managed business school. In the latter, management often overlooks the relevance of staff needs for meaning, purpose and value. This purpose orientation is also where I have previously drawn the line between traditional business schools and humanistic business schools (HUBS) (Amann et al., 2011). A new values-oriented set of institutions might well be emerging. These institutions' philosophies exceed mere commercialisation and profit maximisation, and subsequently penetrate their teaching, research and overall organisational set-up including HR policies and admission guidelines.

Figure 2: Organisational logics of business schools

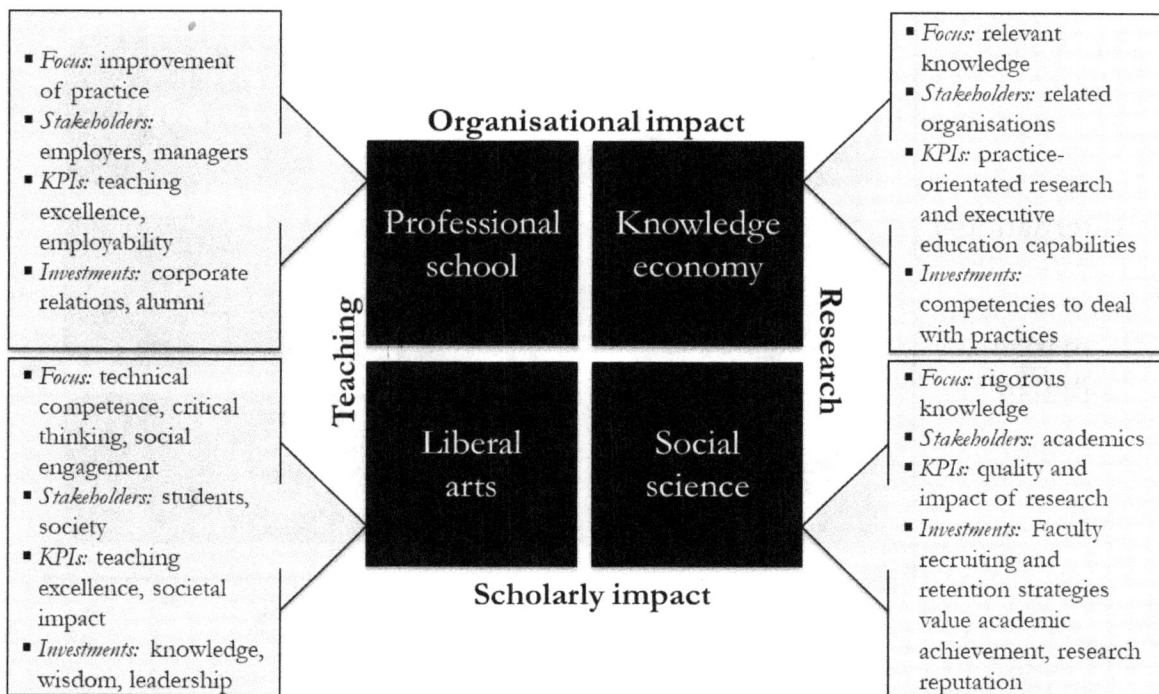

Source: Based on Ivory et al. (2006)

In order to somehow simplify the diversity of business schools, a helpful map emerged from Iniguez de Onzono (2011) who categorises business schools into strategic groups based on two dimensions as the following figure illustrates. The first dimension is the global presence and reputation as indicated, for example, via international accreditations, rankings, the percentage of foreign faculty, students, alliances and locations. The second dimension is the breadth of programmes. Both dimensions span the terrain of schools portrayed in the following figure.

This is a particularly helpful overview, as it clarifies the nature of the rivalry these institutions face, it clarifies the potential next strategic group to join through strategising and it clarifies the types of challenges the dean must cope with. For example, a boutique, such as the top-ranked International

Institute for Management Development (IMD) in Switzerland, has significantly less stakeholders and a simpler business model to run than a school that is active in higher volume undergraduate, high-end graduate, short open, certificate and custom programmes, along with a full-fledged applied and rigorous research portfolio. At the same time, within-country competition and cultural differences persist as Dameron and Duran (2017) detail for the US, Germany, Australia, Spain, Israel, the UK, South Africa, Poland, Canada, Portugal, Sweden and Italy. The next section explores the question: To what extent has the literature detected the plurality and individuality of the dean's tasks?

Figure 3: Strategic groups of business schools

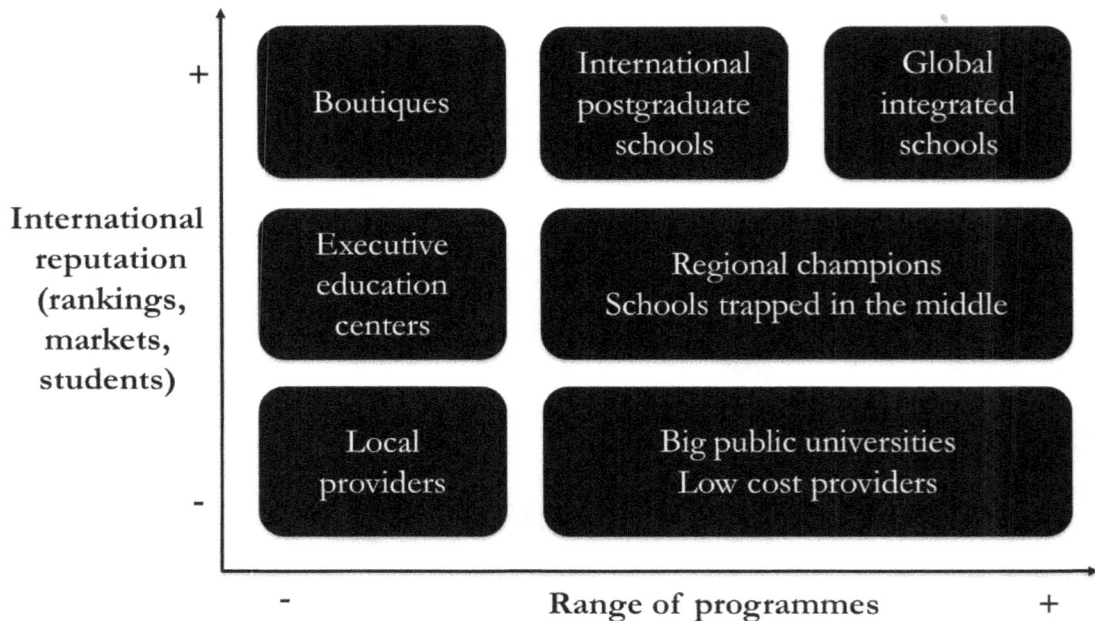

Source: Based on Iniguez de Onzono (2011, p. 70)

This diversity that emerges from the historical developments, the diverging types of schools, the institutions' varying overall purpose and their belonging to a strategic group as outlined above, make it reasonably complicated to define a business school, as their main gestalt and idiosyncrasies diverge easily. Davis (2015) applies the business school notion to "a substantial entity that offers business and management education at degree level" (p. 6). Dawson (2008), in turn, offers a more sophisticated view and definition by defining business schools as a "tri-fold hybrid organisation" (p. 159). Business schools ought to align commercial interests with the interests of the public sector and the demands from professional service partnerships.

Implications of business school types and institutional needs for the role of dean

The section above produces three key insights for the role of deans. Firstly, it is not possible to apply a one-size-fits-all approach to the dean role, as the business school types are too diverse. This renders a standardisation of the role or even a job description impossible. Over time, institutions have paid varying degrees of attention to a local versus a global reach, – or both simultaneously, – showed different degrees of compliance with mainstream Western, i.e. Northern hemisphere, thinking versus diverging alternatives and were equally heterogeneous on the degree of sustainability they emphasized. Then, there are types of schools that demand starkly different outcomes from deans. The Ivory et al. (2006) framework would hold deans accountable differently, such as for actual organisational impact and teaching in a professional school. Juxtaposing this set-up with a social science institution, the dean would have to deliver on the scholarly impact and foster an organisational culture emphasizing and committed to research. Adding Iniguez de Onzono's framework (2011), not four but seven main types of institutions conceivable. A dean operating in a smaller, private but still very international boutique would have to demonstrate more commercial acumen. In turn, a dean at a school that is part of a larger public university set-up would have to deal with a tighter administrative corset, possibly more red tape and with this university an extra stakeholder and, thus, added complexity.

The following assumptions can guide the analysis and show how complicated situational adaptations can get. The international orientation could be either low, medium or high, i.e. three cases. The sustainability orientation could be either low, medium or high, thus considering three cases again. Compliance with Western, i.e. Northern hemisphere, thinking presents three cases (low, medium, high). The overall organisational set-up could comprise four cases, i.e. professional school, knowledge economy, liberal arts or social science. Apart from the international reach, the actual international reputation and organisational size present seven possible cases. The mere review of three business school models could lead to 3x3x3x4x7 finer distinctions equalling 756 cases in which the demands for deans would be notably distinct!

These considerations refer to a static view, which might not necessarily be perfectly realistic in light of the perpetually changing external environments and aforementioned meta-challenges. If one adds a more dynamic view and two additional trains of thoughts, a strong case can be made against a one-size-fits-all approach for the role of deans. There might well be schools without clear strategic orientations or those currently in search of – or already in pursuit of – new strategic orientations as part of transitions (Thomas and Cornuel, 2012).

O'Reilly and Tushman (2004) use the label and concept of the ambidextrous organisation, which is an organisation that focuses on more than one overarching logic. Ambidextrous organisations can, therefore, simultaneously revisit strategies and solutions that had been implemented in the past, while exploring new ideas. This boils down to the dean's role being explored from a situational leadership point of view (see section 2.5 below) instead of a too simplistic one-size-fits-all approach. This analysis is in line with Krahenbuhl (2004) and Bray (2008) noting for the academic context that all institutions and their cultures are de facto different.

2.4. Business school deans and emerging prescribed and proscribed traits

This section includes considerations on the following research fields: 1) apparent ambiguity if not contradictions in the literature when it comes to the role's positioning and scoping within governance systems; 2) analogy-based identity of deans; and 3) dean traits. All these research fields contribute individually to the ensuing summary on the expected traits business school deans ought to portray and develop during their preparation years.

Research field 1: Ambiguity about the dean's role in governance systems

For Davies (2015), the notion of the dean in the business school context refers to "the senior leader of a business school" (p. 6). Elsewhere, Davies and Thomas (2009) also apply the notion of the Chief Executive Officer (CEO) (p. 1398) in tandem with other responsibilities and roles. There is, however, a contradiction in Davies's research: While she views the dean as the senior – even the most senior – leader in the mould of the CEO, her empirical research clearly frames the position as middle management. She relies, thereby, on Floyd and Wooldrige's (1996) framework for middle management assigning the tasks of "synthesizing strategy, facilitating adaptation, championing, and implementing deliberate strategy to explore practices" (Davies, 2015, p. 8) to the dean. Elsewhere and since set-ups are plentiful as the aforementioned typologies of business schools illustrated, the dean may no longer be the senior leader or middle manager but an upper middle manager (Davies, 2016). The following question arises: If a business school's senior leader does not set the strategy but merely facilitates adaptation or implements deliberate strategy, would the notion of senior leader still be accurate? Less clear boundaries and more fluid roles appear to characterise this field.

This governance question of what the dean's role is, represents the first research field identified in the literature. Fagin (1997) views the dean as often in a sandwich position – he or she is "a person and position in the middle" (p. 95). Davies and Thomas (2009) add that the dean's tenure is often limited and, thus, persevering with holistic, long-term change is not the norm. Exploring the governance system further, Davies (2015) also sheds light on the growing number of institutions adding advisory boards as a consequence of their Association to Advance Collegiate Schools of Business (AACSB) accreditations. Davies and Thomas (2009) emphasize that studies usually have a local, national or cultural focus and boundary. Therefore, a contingency theory approach in line with Alajoutsijärvi and Kettunen's (2016) represents a promising avenue forward, positing that a match of the dean's view on the world with the wider university or institutional context predominately determines "appropriateness, survival, and success of deanship" (p. 327) and so does a fit with the local, situational context.

There is a caveat, which does not contradict but elaborates the need to pay attention to each situation individually. The notion of governance may well imply structure, order, division of tasks within clear roles of responsibility and accountability. As Khan (2011) defines it, the notion of governance refers to the processes that are already in place but also to any customs as well as policies that set strategies for the direction of an organisation. In contrast, Wolverton, Wolverton and Gmelch (1999) refer to the academic context as organised anarchy. Van Cleeve (1981) outlines just how challenging it is to manage faculty due to the extremely politically active behaviour. Deans need the skills to operate in such a setting. Fragueiro and Thomas (2011) imply that the dean must be "keeping one step ahead" (p. 205), which boils down to ongoing scans of the environment, diagnosing and legitimising issues and mobilising power.

Thereby, a key challenge is setting boundaries, as the dean operates where the academic and administrative cultures meet (Pruitt & Schwartz, 1999). However, this might just be one area where, situationally, the dean's role might fill voids in a setting that may otherwise be possibly ambiguous. In order to deal with such conditions, a variety of analogies have been proposed as outlined in the following.

Research field 2: Analogy-based identities of deans

Next to the governance lens, the literature includes a string of research on identities that academics often describe via analogies to define this comprehensive and diverse set of roles. Academics emphasize a teleological view. Thereby, the following considerations can pertain to all deans, not only deans of business schools. Tucker and Bryan (1988) share the view that deans are, at times, like doves, dragons or diplomats. Doves are on constant peace-keeping missions due to friction from diverging interests. Dragons defend against threatening forces from inside and outside the organisation. Diplomats know that it is necessary to guide, encourage or persuade staff members.

Picking up on the idea of a multiplicity of roles, Gmelch (2004) likens deans to a Janus face, as deans must strike a balance between the university's or the institutions' interests and the faculty's needs. For Kambil and Budnik (2013), a Janus-faced view would not suffice, since they view deans as having four faces in light of the strategist, catalyst, steward and operator roles they must perform credibly.

These analogies indicate that the dean's role becomes more complex and demanding over time (Starkey & Tiratsoo, 2007). For Symonds (2009), the financial crisis, the ensuing recession, the credit crunch and the overall negatively affected business environments led to an increase in the level of adversity for deans. To name but one example, Davis (2008) outlines that in 2008, a key year in the last major financial crisis, 25% of the UK business school deans have been replaced. O'Reilly (1994) adds that most of the deans apparently fail, as balancing these demands and interests is challenging. Gmelch and Burns (1994) share that deans often appear to end their tenures in a fatigued and stressed out manner. Gmelch et al. (1999) even propose and apply a tool to measure dean stress – the Deans' Stress Inventory (DSI). As an interim summary: The ability to effectively cope with more than one stakeholder group or topic coupled with the ability to resist stress appear to be more or less the explicitly desirable traits of deans. Put differently, deans might well show this skill gap. The following section explores this train of thought separately.

Research field 3: Dean traits

Researchers apply a third lens when they investigate deans: abilities and traits. Arguably, there is a logical overlap with the two preceding lenses, as the ability to fulfil roles within a larger governance system or to effectively act according to an analogy alludes to traits. The discussion on traits in the literature is an explicit one. This is very much in line with the early days of leadership research where trait theory dominated. The argument in the trait theory of leadership is that "personality traits influence leader emergence and effectiveness" (Colbert et al., p. 670). One can expect that subsequent leadership studies will embrace more modern waves within leadership theories, moving beyond leadership as a property of the leader towards leadership as a result of the leader-follower relationship and, most recently, leadership as a social process (Bolden et al., 2013). Bareham (2004) investigates deans and their ability to think strategically, communicate effectively and build internal and external relationships. Williams (2009) similarly focuses on how deans tackle strategic dilemmas and relationship building via a cultural change of the focus areas. Davies and Thomas (2010) emphasize problem-solving, excellence at dealing with issues and people face-to-face, prioritisation and delegation. Gmelch (2004), in turn, prescribes high degrees of adaptability, as there are several transitions to master, such as moving from working in solitary to working in social settings, from focused (on research or teaching) tasks to fragmented, diverse tasks, from having more autonomy to having substantially more accountability, from having a rather private setting to holding a very public position, from writing (rigorous or applied) publications to writing memos or policies, from professing as a professor to convincing and leading, from being in a more stable and controllable environment to being in a more organic one.

In this context, Bray (2008) adds the semantics of prescriptive versus proscriptive norms for deans in academia. While the literature appears to emphasize overporportionally what deans ought to do, – thus the literature prescribes, – scholars pay little attention to proscriptive norms pointing to what deans are expected not to do. Bray discusses a variety of proscriptive norms in a rather unstructured list of don'ts including avoiding unconveyed expectations, insufficiently valuing non-academic staff, avoiding disdain for faculty's demands, regulatory disdain and bending to pressure – as giving in to one group my appear unfair to others.

Moving from proscriptive insights back to prescriptive insights, Kring and Kaplan (2011) extract the following four fields from their research: strategic skills, enterprise management, innovation, as well as people and relationship effectiveness. These four fields are, however, quite broad and almost all-encompassing. One of the areas on people effectiveness is certainly the potential responsibility for faculty management. Instead of focusing on a single style alone, Amann (2017) investigated the leadership versatility of business school deans, arguing that versatility endows an individual with the most flexibility. After all, the dean's role can be comprehensive. The study reveals that 93% of deans regularly exert more than one leadership style. 16% of deans rely on two, 25% on three, 30% on four and 21% on all five of the leadership styles proposed by Cameron and Green (2012). Cameron and Green's framework includes being a thoughtful architect, edgy catalyst, tenacious implementer, visionary motivator or measured connector. Kovaks (2012) adds to this static view the dynamics over time. He outlines that a business school dean's career can comprise various stages with different values, such as the dean potentially starting off as a researcher, course faculty or ambassador, to mention but a few examples. This view refers to not only leadership versatility at one point in time but its adaptation over time.

Interim summary of the insights on business school deans

The sections above review three pertinent research fields on business school deans. Insights to be gained, include the following:

- Research field 1: The ambiguity about the dean's role in governance systems calls for political skills and the ability to deal with complexity, most notably ambiguity as part of complexity within the situational governance setting. This is in line with the preceding analysis that organisations are heterogeneous and that a one-size-fits-all approach would not make sense.

- Research field 2: The section on analogy-based identities of deans, regardless if an author calls for comparisons with biology or Greek mythology or alludes more directly to terms in the leadership literature, suggests that effective deans must first and foremost excel at balancing demands and managing stakeholders. There appears to be a gap between a should-be and an as-is state. Negative stress to the extent of producing fatigue and burnout of deans has been demonstrated in research studies. The analysis differentiates between desirable traits and actual dean profiles.

- Research field 3: Research on dean traits appears to fit perfectly with this line of thinking. Deans must portray versatility – either at one point in time or over time.

As an interim conclusion and in line with Ashby's (2011) logic of requisite variety, the dean fulfils a crucial coping role. Where the school has multiple demands, the dean balances them and moderates across stakeholders. Where the school requires specific action to fulfil its vision, mission and business model, the dean ought to ensure or contribute to alignment. This underlines the importance of sound preparation for their dean roles. Before zooming in on what is known or remains unknown on the leadership development of business school deans, the following two sections provide insights on the more general fields of leadership (2.5) and its development (section 2.6).

2.5. Leadership

First of all, does leadership matter? Several authors have argued their case on the importance of leadership. For example, Andersen and Adams (2016) illustrate and quantify that highly effective leaders lead the highest performing organisations and, in turn, that the low-performance organisations have low-effectiveness leaders. Zenger and Folkman (2014) investigated more than 30,000 leaders on a range of effectiveness criteria, such as employee satisfaction, employee commitment, actual employee turnover or mere intention to quit and satisfaction with pay. They could establish how sound leadership positively impacts these drivers of financial performance and the subsequent actual financials.

Challenges in the leadership literature

A literature review of leadership and leadership development can easily turn into a daunting task. Kellerman (2012) estimates that there are at least 1,400 definitions of leadership and 44 theories contributing to its understanding. Rost (1991), who defines leadership as an influence relationship that exists between a leader and a follower, criticised the absence of a truly integrative and sufficiently holistic framework.

Ciulla (2007) tries to simplify the discussion by pointing out that basically all these definitions argue similarly: Leadership refers to the process in which person A moves person B towards something. Definitions merely diverge on the question of how A manages to accomplish it as well as how A originally decided what needed to be done. Ciulla (2007) equally suggests that we should not become distracted by the less important question of what leadership is but that we should solely focus on what good leadership is. She points to the necessity of emphasizing the business ethics aspect more than mere effectiveness by pointing to what she calls the Hitler problem. Reviewing Hitler, Jimmy Carter and Robin Hood, she discusses individuals with starkly varying degrees of morals and effectiveness.

For Jago (1982), it is not this differentiation between a shared underlying theme of influence or refocusing the discussion on ethics but the clustering of all theories into two groups. On the one hand, there are the universal theories, such as the great man theory viewing leadership as genetic. Another example is trait theory assuming a leader possesses congenital or acquired traits. Universal leadership theories presume that certain behaviours, abilities or features hold under any condition. On the other hand, contingency theories model leadership behaviour as dependent on a given situation, such as the types of followers to lead (cf. Uslu, 2019, for a full review of both streams within the literature).

Goethals and Sorenson (2006) reason there is no general leadership theory regarding the two questions of how person A influences B and how person A came up with the goals in the first place. Even when authors claim boldly, such as Anderson and Adams (2016), that they have made progress in this direction, Adams (2006) warns of a trade-off between synthesis as a priority and the need for openness to surprises, innovations and humility. Palmer (1969) is similarly sensitive to the risk that older approaches of understanding leadership can cause myopia towards newer phenomena and perspectives, as a natural dynamic might cause individuals to fit them to older, better-understood models.

Reams (2016) suggests simplifying the discussion, lowering the expectations and clarifying what an integral perspective actually is. He suggests that any attempt to weave constructs and conceptions together such that they become more accessible, is integrative. Moreover, for him, a case in point is the combined view of leadership effectiveness, which ought to be assessed from multiple perspectives and stakeholders.

Pragmatic approaches to the diverse, fragmented leadership literature

As the leadership field is rich in studies based on divergent schools of thought, there is a need for pragmatism. After all, leadership theories as such are less crucial to the analysis than the process of leadership development per se, which is the focus of the subsequent section 2.6. Furthermore, the purpose of the literature review remains the same: It is about gathering an overview of and reviewing sensitising topics, not about deducting hypotheses based on a constructed conceptual framework.

In order to nonetheless endow the study with such essential sensitising frameworks, three other authors offer a pragmatic view to better structure the leadership field. They include the concept of leadership versatility, main waves within leadership theories, – especially the fifth one currently best labelled as eco-leadership, – and the learning model of leadership.

Firstly, Kaplan and Kaiser (2003) posit that only earlier stages in the development of the leadership field were concerned with identifying definitions, concepts or models. Subsequently, researchers discovered and tweaked typologies until most recently when, as part of situational leadership, leadership versatility emerged as the variable that best explains the individual leaders' and their organisations' performance. This view is particularly relevant, as, in light of the numerous challenges outlined above in the context of business schools and management education, fostering leadership versatility would best enable a dean to perform well situationally, regardless of the challenges and degree of adversity.

Secondly, Western's (2013) descriptive review of discourses on leadership reveals that leadership as a field has progressed categorically in his view as well. Each of the four waves he identifies within the academic literature and theories on leadership represents a holistic, internally consistent and integrated phase of discourse over time. These waves' underlying assumptions and theories within these waves are clearly identifiable. Western's (2013) biggest contribution in light of the sensitising purpose of this first, pre-field work literature review is his big-picture overview of the decades-long research and theorising efforts on leadership. He helps prevent not seeing the forest for the trees, which is a likely risk in light of the aforementioned 1,400+ definitions of leadership. His four waves include the following:

- Wave 1 – leaders as controllers in the early 20th century: The overarching metaphor considers organisations as machines. A scientific approach to conceptualising and measuring drives efficiency and effectiveness. Leaders ought to control for these productivity gains and compliances with set roles and processes. People as followers are a mere means to an end in a starkly dehumanised view of the world although bureaucracy should ensure a minimum of fairness.

- Wave 2 - towards therapists in the 1960s: Addressing precisely this dehumanisation, yet still pursuing ever more effectiveness gains, workplaces were being democratised. Leaders had to learn how to better understand what might be wrong with unmotivated individuals in a clinic-style analysis and subsequent adapted motivation process even if it meant manipulation. The means-to-an-end thinking still dominated and was merely carried out in a more sophisticated manner.

- Wave 3 - towards messiahs in the 1980s: Economically tougher times in the US and Europe along with more globalisation triggered the search for highly charismatic personalities who still enhance productivity and inspire their colleagues. They ought to manage organisational cultures, for example, through their visionary and energising behaviour.

- Wave 4 - towards eco-leaders from 2005 onwards: In light of numerous and recurring scandals, the impact of leaders on society gained more relevance. Sustainability within a larger eco-system started to matter more, as did self-regulation. The attention shifted from leaders as a group to followers. It becomes clear that, as eco-leaders, it is not the leaders' traits or behaviours that truly matter but their actual impact on creating followers and high-performance systems, – thus better eco-systems. This is the essential profile of eco-leadership. This view also led to Kim and Mauborgne's (2014) seminal innovation in the leadership field with their school of thought on blue ocean leadership. Blue ocean leaders have shifted their attention away from themselves, their traits and psychometric test profiles towards a substantially higher engagement, involvement and commitment from their followers. This is helpful when the question arises in this research project of when and how future deans ought to learn these skills to be ready in time.

Thirdly, already decades ago, Bennis and Nanus (1985) viewed the most successful leaders as perpetual learners. Hodgson and White (2001) continued this view of leaders as learners and detailed it for growing uncertainty in business environments. The authors encourage individuals to fully embrace uncertainty, – to even relax in light of it, – as the individuals can learn how to cope with and operate in uncertainty. This view links the field of leadership to identity creation. Gardner (1995) then defined leadership as follow: "leadership is a process in the minds of individuals who live in a culture. Some stories tend to become more predominant in this process, such as stories that provide an adequate and timely sense of identity for individuals" (p.22). Within the learning school of leadership, this identity would consider leaders as learner. Another interesting element of a learning-oriented school of thought within leadership stems from Ancona et al. (2007). In their 4-CAPS model, they achieve three things. They bring an order to numerous leadership capabilities by identifying four central ones (sensemaking, relating, visioning and inventing), which all, in turn, rely on lower-level capabilities in order to clearly explain how a bigger number of capabilities fit into a larger system. They speak of learnable capabilities, yet simultaneously emphasize their praise for the incomplete leader. No individual can master these capabilities and is encouraged to humbly learn more. This insight from the general leadership literature is relevant for business school deans as well. It helps put into perspective the rather undifferentiated call for too many traits being present in deans. Defining leaders as learners is especially conducive in continuation of the argument that a Red Queen effect of being forced to constantly adapt to survive haunts business schools and management education (Iñiguez de Onzoño & Carmona, 2012).

This section 2.5 allowed to gather and review the richness of the leadership field along with its complexity over time. This approach sensitises us to a modern understanding of leadership, which includes the aforementioned versatility, eco-leadership and learning orientation. The following question, which is explored further in the following section, arises: What does the available body of knowledge in the literature contain on leadership development?

2.6. The concept of the leadership pipeline and the emerging gap in the literature

Who is in charge of this learning so that any leader in general or business school deans and their successors in particular can adapt? Is it the aspiring individual who is interested in becoming a dean, for example, or is it the structure in which this individual works, such as a business school? In sociology, scholars referred to this long-lasting question as the structure versus agency debate (Kabele, 2010), which aims at clarifying who really owns the task of developing leadership qualities. This is where the business school and higher education world can learn and benefit from a number of advances made. Not leaving the crucial task of further professional growth and honing of leadership to an employee, a concept labelled as the leadership pipeline became established and gained in popularity.

For decades, the corporate sector has relied on advanced insights and models on how to create leadership pipelines. Initially, Mahler and Wrightnour (1973) suggested key decision points in their crossroads model, which have become more widely used in the corporate sector (Freedman, 2005). Charan et al. (2011, 2001) updated and popularised the model further. The authors distinguish a series of stages or passages that aspiring leaders have to pass successfully. Each of the stages require an individual to spend sufficient time to learn and produce tangible results before being entitled to promotion to the next stage. The authors acknowledge, of course, that organisations might well differ and that not all organisations will fit this scheme perfectly.

Stage 1 foresees individuals spending, for example, a period as a team member after graduating and becoming a new recruit. These team members are individual contributors. They must carry out the tasks in their functional area that management have assigned to them, – be it in marketing or finance to name but two examples, – in the expected time period and at the right quality levels. The first passage takes place once management has identified an individual as promotable, following tangible results. Passage 1 entails a progression from managing self to managing others. Instead of merely being responsible for their own quality of deliverables, these team members adopt team leadership roles. The role that they play in the team and the role that they play for their colleagues start replacing their own professional or technical skills. Certain behaviours have to stop, giving way to new ones, which, in turn, require new learning. These team members start helping others perform, allocate time better and drive home results. Such first-time managers or neophytes (Charan et al., 2011) start to value and not merely tolerate managerial tasks.

If superiors observe evidence of performance in this role, the next passage ensues – from managing others to managing managers. This is when individuals move even further away from carrying out functional tasks themselves and create performance through others, i.e. those who, in turn, lead their subordinates. This is also when more awareness of real strategic issues develops, as the organisational alignment of all teams becomes even more crucial and, for the first time, a real priority.

Passage 3, subsequently, concerns those fewer individuals who still perform at that level move from managing managers to functional manager. Leadership spans grow as an individual becomes responsible for an entire function, such as marketing or procurement. Furthermore, while more direct communication with subordinates was still possible before, it is essential to also reach colleagues who are further down the organisational hierarchy.

Two additional skills include the ability to compete with other functional managers for resources, while simultaneously working well with them across functions. This takes place in a setting where the functional manager usually does not have authority over these other functional managers. Thinking has to become even more strategic and long term.

If performance continues to be positive, the next passage follows. Passage 4 foresees moving from functional manager to business manager. Individuals have to balance even more demands. Certainly by now, individuals face many areas and topics with which they are not familiar. Their learning speed and versatility matter more than ever before, while subject matters become more complicated. If there is success, individuals continue their careers in passage 5 from business manager to group manager and they take charge of several entities. Therefore, these individuals need to learn portfolio management, including dynamic strategising, resource allocation and making tough decisions.

At this stage, individuals also learn how to develop next generation business managers effectively as part of their holistic leadership work. If individuals continue to excel, they ultimately gain promotion to passage 6 – from group manager to enterprise manager. Their thinking must become even more strategic, continuously scanning and influencing business environments, not only downwards in organisational hierarchies. At this level, their tasks and daily contributions are the most remote from the early technical or professional skills that helped them in stage 1.

Critical evaluation and comparison to other models

When it comes to a critical evaluation of the leadership pipeline model, the literature seems to converge and agree easily when it comes to the logic of necessary transformations, such as Burke (2006) and Boal (2000), as tasks inarguably change as outlined by Pietersen (2015). This train of thought posits that past behaviours may well have accounted for a promotion but would not necessarily account for future ones (Goldsmith & Reiter, 2007). Skipping or not completing required adaptations risks derailment and entails substantial cost caused by bad managers (Hogan et al., 2007).

Kaiser (2011) equally underlines the gains in popularity of the concept of leadership pipelines and supports the logic of transitions yet criticizes that the concept represents propositional knowledge only and the empirical foundations are underdeveloped. Hiller et al. (2011) equally point to the predominant focus on organisational needs while it is the individual journey of the at times struggling leader, which requires further investigation and insights. How the unlearning and relearning as part of the ongoing transformation materialises remains underresearched according to Kilner (2015).

There are several additional models that follow this logic of sequentialism, cumulative learning, the need for unlearning and drastic shifts in the value one added to the organisation as summarised in the following table. The number of stages and passages varies somewhat.

One model, which appears to influence several subsequent models, is Freedman's (1998) pathways-and-crossroads model – with only five pathways and four crossroads. Individuals have to face, cope with and negotiate successfully for four 135 degree crossroads, alluding to the drastic, almost 180 degree shifts that ought to take place. According to Freedman (1998), these shifts come in three forms and include a departure from a dated understanding of responsibilities and crucial competencies, a perpetuation of what can be deemed useful and additions of relevant roles and responsibilities.

Table 1: Overview of selected leadership pipeline models

Models	Stages and passages
Charan et al. (2011)	• From managing self to managing others. • From managing others to managing managers. • From managing managers to functional manager. • From functional manager to business manager. • From business manager to group manager. • From group manager to enterprise manager.
Freedman (1998)	• From individual contributor to supervisory manager. • From supervisory manager to manager of a single business. • From manager of a single business to executive manager of a portfolio of several businesses. • From executive manager of several businesses to institutional leader.
Watkins (2009)	• Front-line supervisor to manager of managers. • From manager of managers to function leader. • From function leader to business unit leader. • From business unit leader to group leader. • From group leader to C-level executive.
Rooke and Torbert (2005)	• From opportunist or diplomat to expert. • From expert to achiever. • From achiever to individualist. • From individualist to strategist. • From strategist to alchemist.
Singer (2014)	• From individual contributor to novice manager. • From novice manager to experienced manager. • From experienced manager to transformational leader.
Maxwell (2011)	• From position to permission. • From permission to production. • From production to people development. • From people development to pinnacle.

Andersen and Adams (2016)	• From egocentric to reactive. • From reactive to creative. • From creative to integral. • From integral to unitive.

Rather similar, yet placing less focus on the lower levels in the organisational hierarchy, Watkins (2018) distinguishes clearly between the competency of and traps for the front-line supervisor, manager of managers, function leader (usually a vice-president), unit leader, group leader and, finally, a C-level executive. He emphasizes a key shift that Charan et al. (2011) had, according to him, ignored. Watkins advocates a change of perspectives and skills profiles from managerial science to leadership art. One can easily limit lower-level responsibilities to rules and procedural clarity. At higher levels, other skills, such as pattern recognition, judgment and soft skills including political and emotional intelligence take centre-stage position. Watkins also places special emphasis on the transition from functional manager to business unit leaders, which is where he observes seven seismic shifts that need to take place. Individuals must show successful progress from 1) specialist to generalist, 2) analyst to integrator, 3) tactician to strategist, 4) bricklayer to architect, 5) warrior to diplomat, 6) problem solver to problem finder and 7) role holder to role model.

Singer (2014) differentiates between four stages in a leader's development – individual contributor, novice manager, experienced manager and transformational leader. Rooke and Torbert (2005), in turn, propose seven different manners of leading. They similarly outline what the lower and higher levels of aspirations and leadership qualities are. Their focus, however, is more on the question of how to add more value to the organisation over time and their model zooms in on individual transitions.

A mere opportunist is heavily self-centred and even manipulative. He or she tries to win at all cost. In turn, a diplomat attempts to avoid conflict situations, as belonging to a group and complying with its norms are more important. Experts attempt to apply logic and their expertise. Efficiency matters. One can also describe experts as the individual contributors in Charan et al. (2011) stage 1. Subsequently, the models appear to converge. Rooke and Torbert (2005) envisage achievers who reach goals together with and through teams.

Next, the individualist is able to link personal and company logics. He or she is able to drive strategy and ensure performance across units. The strategist, in turn, excels at even bigger organisational transformations. He or she combines concrete insights with foresights. However, the highest, rarest and most valuable segment consists of alchemists, generating social transformations even beyond the corporate boundaries and integrating materialist and symbolic views. Table 1 above summarises these models.

A different perspective enriches the debate on the leadership pipeline when Maxwell (2011) adds his five levels of leadership. A mere position is the lowest. There are parallels with the team leader position or first leadership role in the models above. The mere title and position can help lead even if the skill level is rather insufficient. The next level, i.e. permission, emphasizes relationship skills. Production deals with the recurring theme of delivering results, as they ensure credibility, influence and legitimacy. Level 4, i.e. people development, underlines the responsibility to take care of successors and build a leadership pipeline. Maxwell (2011) emphasizes that few people reach level 5 – the pinnacle. Here, the author breaks with the logic of a predominantly nurturing view of leadership development (Piaw & Ting, 2014), as he clarifies that this level is only for the naturally gifted.

Simultaneously and somewhat contradictorily, Maxwell also posits that moving up requires further growth and it should be intentional and based on experience. The clear distinction between nature, i.e. natural talent, versus nurture is more blurred than in the other models. Andersen and Adams (2016) integrate the stages of development in their universal leadership approach. They understand that, initially, individuals in stage 1 behave rather egocentrically; in stage 2, they become more reactive and in stage 3 more creative, before advancing to integral behaviour in stage 4 and, lastly, to rather unitive behaviour in stage 5.

The gap in the literature on leadership development of business school deans

A major gap, however, is this very leadership development in business schools, most notably the development of deans. Studies point to the need for efforts in this regard in light of the numerous challenges, but up until now, too few studies followed suit. When Thomas and Thomas (2011) posit that "it is necessary to strengthen and professionalise business schools' leadership" (p. 529), it follows that more research on how to do so and how to prepare current and future deans as leaders must be carried out. Gmelch (2004) outlines a number of transitions when moving into the dean role as outlined above; but how do deans experience their preparation for moving into the dean role?

Davies (2015) similarly concludes that the deanship in business schools remains rather unexplored and calls for more research. She suggests more research on how deans and their schools can provide stronger support for their wider university (peer-to-peer support mechanisms can help provide this support), how actual evidence-based leadership development could materialise and, subsequently, what actual and active career management, also in the form of a business school leadership pipeline, can be like and how it can add value. More voices call for more research on the topic of leadership development of deans. Kraehenbuehl (2004) repeats that deans thus far receive too limited a training for their responsibilities. Bradshaw (2015) investigates the leadership deficit in business schools, which the high turnover of individuals in dean roles aggravates. Davies (2014) also reveals that the average on-the-job experience might be as low as less than three years for half of the deans at UK business schools. In light of the tremendous self-styled tripod of challenges, – more external orientation, innovations in teaching and learning innovations and the need for holistic internal change as outlined above, – how to actually better understand current leadership development is key.

2.7. Critical evaluation and summary of the known and unknowns

This literature review is preliminary in light of the chosen grounded theory approach. For Charmaz (2006, 2012, 2014), the literature review's purpose is to inform the research and the researcher about the key insights and concepts that were applied. An interim conclusion is that the topic has complexity. Amann, Nedophil and Steger (2011) define four drivers of complexity in the DIAF framework – diversity, interdependence, ambiguity and flux. All four render the analysis challenging and also cause adversity for deans:

1. Diversity: There is a diversity of industry trends, types of business schools, business models, leadership concepts, definitions of the dean's role and leadership pipeline models.

2. Interdependence: Factors, such as stakeholder demands and funding opportunities, are interdependent. Industry trends force deans to work on change. Yet, factors need to be aligned to develop thrust. Isolated changes still require changes elsewhere in the organisation, which necessitates holistic thinking.

3. Ambiguity: Short tenures of deans question what impact an individual can have. Individuals often honed different skills, such as skills for teaching or research. Leadership skills might not be as pronounced and consciously pursued as in non-academic corporations.

4. Flux: Industry trends, such as technological change, render past and current solutions outdated at an accelerating pace.

Several main insights and observations emerge before the study continues with more details on the chosen methodology and, subsequently, with the presentation of the empirical findings before theorizing.

If a modern view understands and investigates leadership as a social process (Bolden, Hawkins, Gosling, and Taylor, 2013) as outlined above, one can consider this study as part of leadership as a social process with a special focus on the formation years of effective leaders. To date and to my best knowledge, delving deeper into the literature and discussing the topic within the research context, for example, with Julie Davies while she directed the European Foundation for Management Development (EFMD) International Deans Program that I attended, the leadership pipeline concept has not spilled over from the context of the corporate world to the specific context of business schools. In her report, Davies (2015) details the growing demands on deans and calls for support of a business school leadership pipeline; however, the follow-up is by and large still lacking. There are a few studies that point to the fragmented nature of the manners in which deans onboarded. For example, many deans mentioned that their move into deanship might well have been rather unintentional and even "serendipitous" (Davies 2015, p. 25). There are pointers to transitions, for example, when Gmelch (2004) concludes that many deans struggled when the shift towards being in charge of negotiations and deal-making or, put differently, from their own professing to actually persuading others occurred. However, no integrated framework for holistic leadership talent development appears to be in place.

Studies abound, calling for a revamp of the MBA (Datar et al., 2010), a better future of leadership development in business schools (Canals, 2011), thought leadership actually meeting business needs and particular needs (Lorange, 2008), a greater and faster evolution of the business schools for the 21st century (Thomas et al., 2013), more constructive innovation in business schools (Thomas et al., 2014) and schools from other regions, especially Europe, challenging the dominating US approach towards management education (Durand & Dameron, 2008). However, where are the answers on how to educate those in charge of pathing the way? There is a striking absence of answers and solutions.

The reviewed extant approaches to designing leadership pipelines relate to the corporate world, not business schools. All models share the inherent logic that corporate leaders grow over time. They are not necessarily born, i.e. there is both an opportunity to and a need for leadership development. This logic will also apply in this book when exploring how business school leaders are formed. Therefore, this research takes a clear stance in the nature versus nurture debate on leadership (Piaw and Ting (2014) or as Garic (2006) put it, "development is the key that unlocks the leadership gateway" (p. 19).

In her review, Brown (2001) underlines another necessary switch in perspective. A major contribution is the view of a talent pipeline complementing or even replacing talent pools. One might well perceive talent pools as something that stands still or is even stagnant. Pipelines, instead, have throughput or if something is in the pipeline, she argues, it is more closely associated with the ongoing process. This is in line with Charan et al. (2011) fostering a shift in mindsets away from work to be done towards developmental assignments.

Excelling at a stage should also lead to discussions about qualifying for the next stage instead of cementing an individual's presence in one stage. The passage-oriented models outlined above share a key feature. Their perspective on human beings continue to be traditional although many have criticised business schools exactly for such a dated view. The paradigm in business schools ought to shift away from functionalist, profit and shareholder value towards humanistic schools that foster the United Nations Global Compact Sustainable Development Goals (SDGs). Other authors call for well-being and human dignity (Pirson, 2019). Instead of the big P for performance, not only organisations and their leaders but also leadership development scholars should encourage innovations that suggest approaches to preserve and enhance human dignity as an end in itself, not merely views focused on efficiency and effectiveness. These models share the perspective of how an organization gains the maximum from an individual's potential. Any dignity considerations are strikingly absent. These models neglect a real caring for human beings and colleagues not merely as a means to an end but an end in itself. None of the authors mention these considerations that are so crucial for the zeitgeist of the age of the UN SDGs and PRME demands for management education.

Emerging research question and research objectives

In light of the obvious research gap, the research project at hand addresses the following research question set for this project: How do business school deans experience their leadership development for their roles?

Breaking this question down, it is of interest to learn more about the following questions:

- Who primarily drove this development? Did the deans or did their institutions? Or both?

- Next to driving the process, how have business schools supported the development of deans?

- What should the future of leadership pipeline management for business school deans be like?

Addressing these research questions will allow the following progress towards achieving the research objectives:

1. Create transparency of the current practices for preparing deans in business schools, for example, their career paths at single versus multiple employers, their experience in the corporate sector and, thus, outside of academia, the business school's organisational status as a rather independent unit versus a division of a larger university, etc.

2. Explore the effective splitting of the responsibilities for this leadership development between schools and aspiring individuals.

3. Define crucial skills for deans and identify clear stages in their development.

4. Create actionable knowledge in the form of publishable insights for leadership development in business schools, as well as the type of insights for the researcher's career management and success.

The next section sheds more light on the methodology and method to address the main research question.

3. Methodology

3.1. Rationale for qualitative research

When determining a research methodology and method, Collis and Hussey (2003) advise scholars to create transparency about their research project's underlying assumptions and those assumptions linked to the research objectives and the chosen research question. Quantitative research tests objective theories by investigating the link between variables, while qualitative research explores the meaning ascribed to a social or human problem (Creswell, 2014). Creswell (2014) likewise argues in favour of a qualitative, constructivist approach if the research goal is exploration rather than theory variation and testing. The research question of how business school deans experience leadership development for their roles clearly points to the goal of exploration. Regarding underexplored and rather complex areas, such as the multi-year, multi-dimensional and multi-stage learning and unlearning for effective deans, qualitative discovery captures the rich interdependencies and dynamics at work far easier. This research project is about this meaning, which Creswell (2014) mentions as a decision-making criterion for the research methodology and method.

This insight starts an explicit discussion of this research project's epistemological and ontological assumptions. Can an external observer objectively assess and accurately evaluate the key drivers of learning for a dean in this multi-year development journey without close interaction with those who have experienced the phenomenon? Constructivism, as Jane et al. (2006) outline, denies such a fully or partially objective reality. They argue that reality might well be socially constructed, that individuals subjectively assign meaning to the events and experiences. Subjectivity, therefore, becomes a key element in this research project in terms of both epistemology (the essence of the research subject) and ontology (the methods of learning about this quiddity). Through iterative inquiry and peeling the onion layer by layer, deans can reveal the key steps and drivers in their personal and leadership growth journey. Qualitative inquiry, i.e. delving deep more adequately, matches the research project's needs and the research question's nature.

The alternative, comprising a quest to generalise across individuals by designing a broader and, therefore, more superficial analysis, lies beyond this research project's scope. It does not match the fundamental assumption that a dean's leadership journey is a subjective experience. It is also possible to deem the very reality accounting for a dean's learning as socially constructed, thus comprising "as many such constructions as there are individuals (although clearly many constructions will be shared)" (Guba & Lincoln, 1989, p. 43). Assigning high importance to meaning also relates to axiology. With sufficient opportunities to explore this meaning, the research project can focus on value and "values of being, about what human states are to be valued simply because of what they are" (Heron & Reason, 1997, p. 287). A dean's career can comprise stages over time, reflecting evolutions in values (Kovaks, 2012). In-depth, qualitative and meaning-orientated research captures that which is valued adequately. Discovering this value and the related dynamics is one of the research objectives. Within qualitative research, there are multiple options for discovering this value, which Starks and Trinidad (2007) detail and outline below. The research question embedded in the corresponding assumptions, thus, becomes the guiding criterion.

3.2. The case for grounded theory

Grounded theory emerges as an approach with substantial potential for how-based research questions. Miller and Fredericks (1999) indicate that grounded theory emerged as a "paradigm of choice" (p. 538) for qualitative researchers. Thomas and James (2006) agree, commenting that, historically, "there can be little doubt that it has been a major - perhaps the major - contributor to the acceptance of the legitimacy of qualitative methods in applied social research" (p. 767). Grounded theory is particularly suitable for analysing concepts grounded in data and when preparing "an explanatory theory of social processes" (Starks & Trinidad, 2007, p. 1373).

In their overview of qualitative research methods, Starks and Trinidad (2007) clarify, for example, that, as an alternative, discourse analysis prioritises the manner in which language helps achieve outcomes, be it on the personal or larger social entity level. According to the authors, this is in contrast to grounded theory, which produces an explanatory theory of selected processes in a specific social setting. However, this scrutiny of discourses is not the scope and focus of the research project at hand, which would contradict the use of discourse analysis as an approach. Instead, grounded theory can clarify research questions dealing with phenomena, such as how a fundamental social process X (in this research project, the forming of deans as business school leaders) can unfold in a specific environment.

The reasoning, accordingly, is in line with Starks and Trinidad's (2007) clarification of grounded theory taking place via researching participants with direct experience of the phenomenon. Exploring multiple settings, thus more than only one in a single-setting case study, generates many more diverse and richer data for the sought-after theory grounded in data. Section 2.3 of the literature review already alluded to starkly different types of institutions and settings likely to be observed, contingent upon the school's emphasis on teaching versus research and scholarly versus organisational impact. Eisenhardt (1989) clarified from her perspective that case studies can serve both the construction of a theory and its testing. Case studies can serve deductive and inductive research alike. However, scholars emphatically state that maintaining the richer cases for longer in the data analysis is the power of a single case study (Siggelkow, 2007), which is in contrast to the reductionist multi-step coding and categorisation process that grounded theory emphasizes. The starting point of both the case method and grounded theory might well be identical in the form of individual cases. As these richer descriptions in the form of extensive narratives (Eisenhardt & Graebner, 2007) in case or caselette form on deans in their unity are not part of the research goals of this study, I did not pursue the case study method further. These narratives might, however, represent a promising avenue for future research, since they can complement grounded theory as Gregory et al. (2013), as well as Gregory et al. (2015), illustrate.

Furthermore, I excluded action research from the list of potential research methods, as the primary research goal was understanding, – not immediately improving, – action. While I carried out this research in part to support the preparation of future deans in business schools, this stage focuses on exploration. The formation process of becoming a dean can easily cover one or several decades. Action research's spiral process of investigating an issue, acting upon gained insights and subsequent fact-finding goals as Lesha (2014) describes in educational contexts, represent a misfit with the research goal and assumed periods.

Zooming in on constructivist grounded theory

When studying business schools' leadership pipelines, this research project opts for a more modern, iterative and flexible approach to grounded theory in accordance with that of Charmaz (2014). In their review of the field of ground theory, Ramalho et al. (2015) identify three waves within the grounded theory movement. They include Glaser and Strauss' (1967) classic or traditional approach, which Glaser (1992) refined while perpetuating its dominant logic. Strauss (1987) and Corbin (1990) added what Ramalho et al. (2015) but also Mills et al. (2008) refer to as evolved grounded theory method. As a student of Glaser and Strauss, Charmaz (2000) added a third approach – the constructivist version.

Parry (2003) warns that new researchers could find the diversity of grounded theory versions overwhelming. Morse and Niehaus (2009) map symbolic interactionist grounded theory, Glaserian grounded theory, situational analysis with dimensional analysis and constructivist analysis as potential versions. Charmaz (2016) explains that her constructivist grounded theory builds on clear, non-objectivist assumptions. Constructivist grounded theory aims at discovering the meaning in data, not uncovering reality which would be more objectively available to all researchers on a topic. Grounded theory understands that not only the data as such but the process of analysis matter. Lincoln et al. (2011) argue similarly by seeing knowledge as co-constructed by the researcher and the interactions with the context, such as the interviewees. Therefore, proximity to those that experience the phenomenon is key. Simultaneously, it is acceptable in constructivist grounded theory that this data analysis is characteristic of the researcher's idiosyncratic thinking, as the sense is not exclusively in the data.

In line with Charmaz (2014) opining that the resulting theory as dependent on the researcher's view, I also acknowledge the importance of the researcher and individual interests and preferences during research, such as avoiding a too tight corset of objectivist rules when creating meaning. Adding one's individuality when interpreting complex phenomena, such as the development of deans, can create richer and more diverse sets of frameworks. The literature review in Chapter 2 provided a summary of the main complexity drivers concerning the development of deans and concluded that it is indeed complex.

Substantive versus formal grounded theories

In the context of grounded theory, Glaser and Strauss (1967) see room for a pair of theories – a substantive theory remains rather context-specific, its alternative formal theory becomes generic. Sense-making and driving the development of a new context-specific substantive theory grounded in data is based on co-created meaning. Other researchers are likely to have read other studies or would manage to gain access to different study participants for a subsequently diverging coding process. As an interim summary and ontologically, quantitative or objectivist research assumes that reality as such exists regardless of and independent from an individual's perception and interpretation (Ormston et al., 2014). This is mirrored in this study. Epistemologically and clarifying how to learn more about self-styled reality, truth is co-created in the very inquiry and probing during the interviews, and during the coding and interpretation.

Strict rules versus flexibility in constructivist grounded theory

Charmaz (2006) similarly encourages researchers not to understand coding guidelines as a tight corset and an overly rigid process that must be followed meticulously. There is flexibility as long as key steps of open and focused coding data, ongoing memo writing to capture observations, insights, categories, further theoretical sampling and an integration of the overall analysis take place (Charmaz, 2012). Her earlier publications, Charmaz (2000) and Charmaz (2006), detailed more steps. The core of these steps that are identical across sources (cf., for example, Sbaraini et al., 2011, Tie et al., 2019) include commencing by an initial coding and categorising, supporting and advancing the analysis by compiling memos, then continuing the data gathering as well as analysis with the constant comparative method, adding theoretical sampling, ensuring theoretical sensitivity, embarking on more focused and axial codes before identifying core categories, further abducting theoretical codes and finalisation of the theorising. Her approach does not necessarily overlap perfectly with others, which, in turn, show heterogeneity as Ralph et al. (2015) suggest. There is a need to clarify, which is an approach that is followed in any research process.

3.3. Interviews as data collection method

Charmaz (2012) understands interviews as "unassailable" (p. 676) in grounded theory and several researchers argue congruently, such as Mruck and May (2007) who illustrate how interviews can trigger valuable reflections among interviewees. Heizman (2003) goes further, arguing that the real value of interviews is in the potential to capture relevant and revealing non-verbal communication.

As for the specific context of deans in business schools, interviews can flexibly accommodate the diversity of individual career paths as antecedents, traits, behaviours and dynamics, as well as accommodate the various roles that deans of business schools might play as role models in different schools (Kovaks, 2012). This explicitly addresses aspects of a more fundamental debate on nature versus nurture in business school leadership. Research will also shed light on the long-lasting discussion in sociology whether the structure, – in other words, the business school as an organisation, - or the agent (Kabele, 2010) owns the task of developing leadership qualities. My personal interest in what study participants have to share further strengthened the choice for interviews. In line with Riessman (2008), interviews in grounded theory allow for studying what kind of stories study participants have to tell, how they share them, what makes them tick and why the stories are told in a specific manner. Riessman (2009) likewise argues that the category-centeredness in grounded theory can be advanced with interviews as part of the constant comparison method. This can lead to substantially more in-depth information being shared than in a text-based, remotely administered, anonymous survey, for example.

Supporting secondary data analysis with the help of online CVs, which are, for example, available on business schools' and social media's websites, such as LinkedIn.com, bolsters the pre-interview information process but is more factual than experiential. Put differently, online CVs mention a career's formal elements (if deemed accurate) but might be incomplete regarding the real sources of experiences for subsequent leadership skills. Interviews are a better method of obtaining a higher level of information richness (Cassell, 2009). Cohen et al. (2011) maintain that interviews have a long tradition in education research and explain that interviews can even achieve a solid information depth in shorter timeframes.

These interviews need to be on a 1:1 basis and should not be group interviews. The latter are less relevant, as the study participant is an individual whose experiences the interviewer needs to explore actively, such that more opportunities to probe arise (Holstein & Gubrium, 2004). Opdenakker (2006) distinguishes between various interview styles ranging from structured, semi-structured and unstructured versions, which point to a series of interviewer effects. Interviewers can use semi-structured interviews (see below) to research rich descriptions of what may be a decades-long personal development journey.

These interviews must be sufficiently flexible to incorporate critical incidents (Torres et al., 2015), which might be very personal and difficult for the interviewer to anticipate. A too rigid interview set-up might well be counterproductive. For grounded theory, the literature suggests types of questions, such as Wright and Leahey's (2013) research that exemplifies circular types of questions. Charmaz (2012) shares numerous examples of conducive options, too. Before embarking on interviews, I familiarised myself with them, along with the categories of interviewer effects and suggested coping strategies (cf. West & Blom, 2016).

3.4. On sampling, pursuing sampling adequacy and theoretical sufficiency

As outlined in the introduction section 1.1., I know my employment context rather well after years of working in it. There is curiosity in other contexts, in reaching in-depth insights from those that have experienced the phenomenon both in terms of compliance with the method but also to satisfy the thirst for learning. Therefore, the process of choosing interviewees had to reach beyond my employer. This impacted on my study design. I chose to adopt an approach to interviews based on the exchange of ideas with the study participants. Building on an exchange theoretical perspective, Van Maanen (1991) points to an innate, authentic curiosity in an interviewee that can foster an engagement and participation in the exchange process. Gaining an opportunity to reflect can increase the likelihood of participation and openly sharing crucial information. Interviewees might realize both the necessity and opportunity to practice reflexivity. In turn, I read up on bracketing as outlined by Fischer (2008) as own preconceptions should not impede me from gaining new insights. Bracketing is important in spite of the ample space for subjectivity in constructivist grounded theory, in which the researcher adds uniqueness to the research process.

In line with Sbaraini et al. (2011), this study combines an initial purposive and subsequent theoretical sampling approach. Purposive sampling started with the original focus on the MENA region in mind. All PRME member signatory institutions listed on the PRME website together with their email addresses were selected and their dean was identified from the submitted PRME progress report that is available online or by reviewing these business schools' websites. They were approached via email. Yet, as a result of slow progress in negotiating access, the geographic scope was expanded to include Europe where my employer is headquartered although I am not based in Europe. This might well enable more access than would otherwise be the case, for example, when compared to Latin America, Australia or New Zealand. This is in line with research being in need of pragmatism and not losing sight of what is possible (Blaxter et al., 2006).

There is an additional layer of motivation for this next to the MENA region being underresearched from a business school leadership perspective. The MENA region and subsequently Europe would be the most interesting contexts to study in light of my current employment at a French business school and delivering programs in the Arab world. Regarding the type of schools, I focus on the deans of the signatory schools of the United Nations Global Compact PRME Initiative. By becoming a PRME signatory institution, these schools show their commitment to better, broader values and a positive impact on society. Nevertheless, implementing PRME is also challenging. Solitander et al. (2012) clarify that it can be demanding if business schools go beyond superficial, misleading window dressing, achieving holistic, school-wide change in order to be an organisational role model.

Why is there a focus on PRME member organisations? PRME requires regular reporting on key performance indicators and continuous improvement initiatives. PRME signatory business schools are, therefore, an interesting research target group for the following reasons: Business schools demand more corporate social responsibility (CSR) from companies and their alumni. In turn, these schools need to achieve similar expectations. Beyond commercial viability, effective teaching and research, they should also deliver on the normative level. In line with Mehta (2011), it is also necessary to implement CSR in business schools, which would augment the level of deliverables that, beyond creating research output, will offer individuals an education and provide the labour market with trained graduates.

PRME signatory schools have higher expectations of leaders because the goal system is more diverse. As tasks, the role of effective leadership and the reviewing of the leadership pipeline matter more, given the high expectations. The expectations require schools to adhere to six main principles and report on the ongoing improvements in order to render their offering and operations more responsible (Forray et al., 2015). The signatory schools, therefore, accept higher responsibilities, stakeholder demands and internal workloads to comply with the principles – as well as continuous improvement initiatives over time. To conclude, the higher the demands based on the published six principles of responsible management education, the stronger the emphasis should be on growing the right talent and developing the right leaders for these business schools. These leaders must not only build a solid foundation for career advancement through their academic work but should also show leadership potential and hone the corresponding skills. They are committed to exhibiting a warm heart and care about their larger responsibilities. This broader set of expectations demands more from the established leadership development paths.

The aforementioned perspective that research requires pragmatism and cannot lose sight of what is feasible as suggested by Blaxter et al. (2006), views another argument entering the fray and speaking in favour of relying on PRME. I have participated in PRME events internationally for more than ten years as part of the working group on anti-corruption. While I did not know any of the interviewees or other approached candidates personally, – as working group members are usually individuals below the business school leadership and dean level, – it can be a factor that can foster trust at the beginning of the interviews. Denzin and Lincoln (2000) argue it is essential to build rapport with interviewees and become acquainted as much as possible. Zakaria and Hatib bin Musta'amal (2014) clarify that sharing commonalities can achieve this goal and enable a better information flow and more mutual trust.

Theoretical sampling

As outlined above, the empirical study started off with a purposive sampling approach by interviewing business school deans, – thus, those who have experienced the phenomenon of preparing for their tenure in one way or another. As exemplified by Sbaraini et al. (2011), theoretical sampling was added later. Theoretical sampling continued to rely on the same pool of deans of PRME signatory institutions interested in participating in the study. Particular attention was paid to their ability to substantiate, disconfirm or complement previously emerging codes. Thus, criteria for further theoretical sampling did not alter the nature of groups but influenced the sought-after content. In line with Sbaraini et al. (2011), filling gaps, overcoming ambiguities, substantiating and enriching – or countering – previously coded observations and developed categories characterised the subsequent part of the interviews with the ultimate goal of the new theory in mind. This is perfectly congruent with Charmaz (2012) as the main overall blueprint to carry out this analysis.

In the aforementioned categories, a variety of illustrations, drivers, motives, reasons or materialisations are added to the analysis to ensure richer descriptions and working towards a true *understanding* of the phenomenon. Constant comparisons of quotes, codes and categories continued until sufficiency was deemed to have been reached. Probing took place with subsequent interviewees and previous quotes were reread to explore how and where they fit.

One of the grounded theory's particularities is the uncertainty about how many interviewees to target and when to discontinue the interviews. According to Stern (2007), sampling and interviewing ought to continue until saturation is achieved. This is also true for very small numbers of interviews. In a review of 100 grounded theory-orientated studies, Thomson (2011) explains that the studies relied on between 5 and 114 interviewees, with an average of 25 interviewees. 22% of the published research used more than 31 interviewees, 33% relied on 20-30 respondents, 32% on 10-19 and 12% used fewer than 10 interviewees. Morse (2000) adds two more dynamics by observing that there "is an inverse relationship between the amount of usable data obtained from each participant and the number of participants" (p. 4) and that the more data a researcher gains from one interviewee, the fewer are the participants whom the researcher needs.

Such statistics can provide a rough overview, but it is not possible to pre-determine the sample size before the data collection and analysis (Corbin & Strauss, 1998) because the data dictate the sample size situationally. Consequently, researchers cannot generally predetermine or assess sample sizes as large or large enough beforehand. This inability leads to researchers combining sampling, subsequent data collection and the data analysis (Baker & Edwards, 2012). Mason (2010) qualifies this guideline further by clarifying that sample sizes and the quest for saturation link to the research objectives and quality of the data obtained from the interviewees. Moreover, Glaser and Strauss (1967), as well as Strauss and Corbin (2012), maintain that smaller and reduced sample sizes are possible and effective if the researchers select the right participants as key informants, which this study aimed to.

The quality of the interviewer's skills also matters to ensure that the data's quality is sufficient. In the context of this study, the identification of key patterns is very important in respect of patterns that are congruent and incongruent with the leadership pipeline concept in the corporate sectors. Bowen (2008), therefore, contends that sampling should primarily focus on sampling adequacy – generalisability or representativeness are not priorities. Saturation is clearly a judgement call (Thorne & Darbyshire, 2005), subjective and, according to Dey (1999), also imprecise. Researchers very often declare saturation without sufficient evidence or without proving it (Morse, 2011), although the positivist language of proving could be ill-placed in qualitative research.

Charmaz (2006) clarifies just how important saturation is in grounded theory. She agrees with Dey's (1999) argument that theoretical sufficiency adequately describes frequent approaches to grounded theory. Theoretical sufficiency refers to the phenomenon that, instead of data saturating categories, researchers arrive at categories that the data merely suggest as a more pragmatic and efficient approach to grounded theory. This approach bears the risk that a too superficial analysis is likely to affect a study's value and legitimacy. Grounded theorist studies should be aware of these risks and should be sufficiently transparent regarding how the researchers tackled them.

Implementation of interviews

"Research is the art of the feasible" (Blaxter et al., 2006, p. 157). This insight influenced the interview design and implementation process. In June 2017, a pervasive blockade surprised Qatar (Zafirov, 2017) where I reside. A group of other MENA countries froze their trade with Qatar and suspended direct flights. In order to proceed pragmatically with the research project, I had to conduct the interviews in different modes: in person whenever possible, for example, during major conferences such as the Academy of Management, but alternatively via Zoom, a sufficiently high-quality teleconferencing system. Several governments in the region, such as the United Arab Emirates (UAE) and Qatar, continue to block Skype, which could have been a software alternative. As theoretical sufficiency was not reached after the initial set of interviews that could be organised, the regional scope broadened to include Europe while maintaining the focus on PRME institutions.

This study applied an open-structured, open-question approach to ensure flexibility in order to pursue emerging topics and probe them when needed. Very few warm-up questions were used, which served more as conversation starters than a tighter corset of questions. Sample questions included topics, such as when someone decided to become a dean, whether this was part of a longer-term plan, if the interviewee underwent active preparation and what the main source of learning was prior to the deanship challenges. The emphasis was on allowing the interviewees plenty of space and time to go beyond these questions and share any information relevant to them.

Eventually, 15 interviews with current business school deans of PRME signatory institutions were needed to arrive at theoretical sufficiency. Interviews lasted between 45 minutes to three hours. The interviews ended having all questions clarified and gaining a clear picture of each individual case. Further probing continued with follow-up questions for subsequent interviewee. Six of them resided in four different countries in the MENA region (Middle East and Northern Africa). The other nine deans worked in six different Western European countries at the time of the interview. In order to ensure confidentiality and anonymity as documented in the ethics approval for this study and as agreed upon with the interviewees, further location details are omitted in the following. They matter less for the analysis than the patterns of leadership development they had to share. The next section delves deeper into which ethical challenges were anticipated and how they were mitigated.

Reflections on interviewer biases and bracketing as a coping mechanism

The researcher's role in constructivist grounded theory differs starkly from the one in objectivist grounded theory. The researcher aims for more proximity and plays a key role in assigning meaning. This also applied in my case, as I inquire about what they had done to prepare, what the most helpful steps were, what they wished they had done, what catalyser and inhibitors were present and how they drove their development in relation to the employers' helpfulness. There are potential biases emerging as Singh and Estefan's (2018) suggest. The authors share that within this approach, the researchers, – i.e. my values and interests, – enter the fray and that the researcher actively and passionately engages when entering into the discourse with the study participant. This emphasizes the importance of being aware of interviewer effects and shows higher degrees of reflexivity.

To name but two, position and attribution effects can easily materialise in a study like this one, which is carried out as part of a lifelong learning initiative as well as career planning to prepare for a potential deanship later on. A certain admiration for individuals having accomplished what I aspire to appears natural and human. As Berger (2015) reasons, it is not uncommon that a researcher's beliefs have an impact. Bracketing, as Fischer (2008) details, represents a process of identifying and temporarily setting aside one's own assumptions. Reading up on bracketing and interviewer assumptions and biases, I remained sensitive to the risks and aimed at remaining as open as possible during the interview process.

3.5. Coding approach

Charmaz (2012) inspires the grounded theorising process applied in this research project. She exemplified both the process as well as the reporting depth in a sample study of hers. Simultaneously, I consulted other studies to ensure congruence with possible, additional developments in the field, such as Tie et al. (2019), Breckenridge et al. (2012), Sbaraini et al. (2011) or Mills et al. (2006). Next to this group of publications on the how-to of constructive grounded theory, I scrutinised comparable in-depth studies applying the method such as Lassig (2012) or Ford (2010) to learn more about preparation, execution and reporting practices. This allows for building up more knowledge on the topic the more illustrative studies become available.

Following Charmaz's (2012) suggested process of initiating the analysis with key informants (Rousseau, 1990), the first step in coding was a line-by-line coding of the typed-up interview notes, thereby relying on active language and gerunds, such as "exploring", "stopping" and "rethinking". This emphasizes a process within a larger set of dynamics. While, during the interview, mind maps secured the themes and quotes and also ensured that the flow of the discussion with the interviewee was documented. Subsequent typing up in Microsoft Word captured the text and content for further analysis, together with the memos. Handwritten quotes on a printout described responses and addressed Glaser's (2004) key question in grounded theory about what really happens in the data.

Focused coding followed with the aim of identifying more abstract, incisive codes or categories, which might well integrate responses from more than one interviewee (Charmaz, 2012). Each interviewee was assigned a code, – also to protect anonymity, – with I1 referring to the first interviewee, I2 to the second, etc. Emerging categories guided probing in further interviews and could, if substantiated in constant comparisons of preceding and subsequent interviews, eventually help build the theoretical framework. Special attention was paid to retaining a certain degree of flexibility such that new themes could still emerge and there is not a too dominant approach of a path dependency during the interviews. However, emerging categories turned out to be rather robust. Variations primarily stem from individual CVs or organisational settings, while still fitting with the overall skeleton or structure of crystallising categories. Emerging categories included non-linearity, non-desirability, non-specificity, non-sequentialism or non-stockability and non-existence. The prefix non intends to underline the deviation from the concept of leadership pipeline.

3.6. Memo writing approach

Memo writing helps capture impressions, support contemplation and prepare leaps when it comes to bridging codes and more abstract concepts in category form as outlined by Birks et al. (2008). These authors agree that working with memos is a reasonably flexible approach employed by novice and more senior researchers. Memo writing was omnipresent throughout the entire research project. Next to writing notes on paper, text was dictated via dictation software (Dragon NaturallySpeaking). Frequently, diagrams were drawn to depict connections amongst codes and contexts. Memos were compiled at the end of each interview and regularly throughout the entire process.

Hennink et al. (2017) differentiates between the impressions created by hearing the insights beforehand versus understanding all of them after having heard them. For Hennink et al., reaching one of these insights would already be enough while Morse (2015) sets higher bars and expects researchers to reach both the insights and the understandings. This research project, in contrast, adopted a theoretical sufficiency approach – continuing the interviews until sufficient data as input could be gathered such that grounded theorising can be enabled and concluded. The subsequent section 4.4 sheds light on theoretical sampling.

3.7. Integrating the analysis and subsequent discussion with extant literature

This section outlines two key insights for the phase of integrating the emerging categories, which are in turn based on the codes from the interviews. Firstly, the approach complies with the recommendation of Chandrasegaran et al. (2017) who suggest visualisations to support theorising. Such visualisation or diagramming might well be one of the few elements shared across various grounded theory approaches (Strauss & Corbin, 1990).

Secondly, it is helpful to revisit the importance of analogies when theorising. Leadership pipelines utilise an analogy, the analogy of a technical, physical pipeline with stages, and the grounded theory might well benefit from relying on an analogy too. This is very much in line with Ketokivi et al.'s (2017) analysis who argue that an emerging, single analogy can represent a culmination of this integration.

Section 4.7. describes the result of the integration of categories developed in section 4.2. through to section 4.6. Thereafter, section 4.8. discussed the emerging grounded theory with extant literature. McGhee et al. (2007) aim to ensure that researchers portray and practice reflexivity such that prior knowledge would not distort the construction of a fresh theory grounded solely in data. Reviewing primarily the types of business schools and their challenges, past insights on the role of deans and the concept of the leadership pipeline from within the field of leadership rendered me sensitive to ask better questions and identify convergences as well as divergences from the established body of knowledge. Section 4.8. adds more distinct reviews to the analysis of the grounded theory. This can enable hypotheses for future empirical testing. However, the scope of this research project is clearly limited to a better understanding of the phenomenon as outlined in the research objectives detailed in section 1.1. The final chapter on conclusions hints at possibly taking the analysis empirically further and quantitatively test gained insights as an effort towards generalisation.

3.8. Management of ethical issues

According to Ritzer (2015), it is possible to address legitimacy and moral authority via honest attempts to deal with potential ethical challenges that could influence research projects. This research envisages the study of organizations other than the researcher's employer. This approach avoids the guilty knowledge phenomenon, which might emerge when carrying out research in the researcher's individual backyard (Williams, 2009, p. 212).

In this context, Bulmer (1987) clarifies that ethics refer to principled sensitivity regarding others' rights and the view of humans; not as means to an end but an end in themselves. In order to address this principled sensitivity, Christians (2000) outlines four pillars: strict avoidance of deception and truly informed consent, confidentiality and accurate reporting.

Regarding informed consent and the avoidance of deception, other research methodology experts, such as Cohen et al. (2011), agree about the importance of obtaining interviewees' informed consent as a crucial step in minimising research projects' ethical weaknesses. Such consent was easy to obtain for the following reasons: Besides an industry-wide consensus that change is happening, PRME is still new and has too few routines and little experience. Deans might then be expected to welcome opportunities to reflect on how to prepare for the challenges and whether they are prepared for these. I proactively shared that learning more about leadership development for the dean role can be beneficial for future generations of candidates for the dean role. Furthermore, in the PRME community of which the book author is a member, there is a positive, open culture of cooperation, transparency and interest in continuous and never-ending improvement and also in the further professionalisation of business schools. This explicitly includes leadership development.

Christians (2000) also encourages researchers to address confidentiality proactively. While schools cooperate in PRME-related initiatives, they might well compete in parts of their operations, for example, for regional research funds, faculty and student talent. On a more personal level, business school deans might be interested in moving to other schools in the region and beyond – a potential interest to protect. Therefore, the book author guarantees the interviewees' anonymity and confidentiality. A final, explicit and written informed-consent release process was in place to ensure that the interviewees agreed with the level of analysis and publication (See the appendix for the UoL ethics approval).

Christians (2000) continues his quality criteria by emphasizing professional data collection and analysis. Huber and Power (1985) posit that, at times, study participants honestly cannot remember. I tried to anticipate this, at least partially, by reviewing online CVs, for example, on LinkedIn or on the business school websites. Also, I acted in line with Strauss and Corbin's (1998) advice that researchers should adhere to open, axial and selective coding. Initially, diagramming should create visual representations of the emerging themes, which Charmaz (2014) suggests in the context of grounded theory studies. Observations were discussed with subsequent interviewees. Emerging themes and clusters of key topics lead to categories that researchers can analyse in a subsequent template analysis (Waring & Wainwright, 2008). A template analysis can help simplify cross-interview comparisons and saturation (Charmaz, 2014).

Ensuring that the research builds on the right skills, helps minimise mistakes. Emerging patterns enable an identification of leadership plateaus and transitions that deans need to master. These plateaus and transitions increase the likelihood of them achieving promotions and succeeding at subsequent levels, which is in line with the aforementioned logic of holistic career management and leadership pipelines. These steps reflect this book's positive intentions and, – as Blaxter et al. (2006) outline, – avoidance of conflicts of interest, both of which are key in research projects.

3.9. Summary of the research design and critical evaluation of the chosen methodology and method

To address the research question of how business school deans experience leadership development for their roles, I opted for a qualitative research design and constructivist grounded theory to explore the phenomenon and work towards an explanatory framework. Constructivist grounded theory presumes that the researcher plays a key role in this abductive reasoning process, as a subjective lens does not merely discover meaning in objective data. The sense is not only in the data but mirrors the individuality and personal value added by each researcher. This turns the researcher from a mere conduit into a real creator of meaning, justifying why someone specific should be involved in the research. My own interests in learning more about the topic, along with what I have read and experienced, render me uniquely motivated to carry out this study and produce tangible results. This might involve my positive biases of valuing a PRME orientation and continuous improvement of processes in business schools, but also relevant and actionable knowledge, more than might otherwise be the case.

Making interviews the method of choice complies with the demands of constructivist grounded theory due to the possibility of becoming better acquainted with and learning directly from those who have experienced the phenomenon. Interviews were to continue until theoretical sufficiency could be achieved, meaning until sufficient interviews were carried out to start and finalise a first explanatory theory grounded in the data. PRME schools are particularly relevant, due to their focus on values and the added adversity this might cause. I opted for a variety of international settings in order to take context-specific differences into account.

Beyond my personal assumptions and preferences regarding carrying out research and, therefore, very much in line with what the literature on research suggests, I identified grounded theory for the how-based research question after I had scrutinised the literature for a suitable approach, deciding in favour of it and arguing against other options as outlined above. Starks and Trinidad's (2007) differentiation between three different qualitative approaches helped establish the link between the research question and grounded theory. These authors provide a clear argument for grounded theory fitting the book's research question. Starks and Trinidad outline that grounded theory enables the discovery of theory via an examination of concepts based on how they are grounded in data and a subsequent explanatory theory of a particular and chosen process within a social setting (Starks & Trinidad, 2007). These scholars also clarify how a basic social process X, such as leadership development, can occur in context Y, such as a business school. Other qualitative approaches, such as phenomenology and discourse analysis, pursue different research goals, which the authors outlined in their detailed review.

Having identified and fixed grounded theory as an approach for this book it was crucial to fully comprehend grounded theory before relying on it further. Glaser (2016) outlines that grounded theory is a suitable approach for research at all levels, as it almost automatically leads to the production of original contributions. Commenting on grounded theory, Thomas and James (2006) argue that grounded theory might well have been the major contributor towards the acceptance and legitimisation of qualitative methods within applied social research.

Limitations of the chosen research design

There are, however, drawbacks to grounded theory. Firstly, there are different schools of thought in terms of grounded theory, which leads to ambiguity regarding the approach referred to. Since the approach apparently still evolves and since it is not a static approach, these factors complicate the application of grounded theory. Charmaz (2006), to mention only one example, outlines how scholars have packed different meanings, definitions, assumptions and competing versions under this label. In her 2006 study, she views grounded theory as fluid, flexible, pragmatic and strongly contingent upon the researcher's engagement with the research process and the data. In her 2014 study, she argues in favour of an even more flexible constructivist approach to grounded theory.

In contrast to this rather constructivist version, Glaser (1978), especially in the earlier days, emphasized its positivistic, objectivist antecedents. In 2001, by zooming in on a specific detail, Glaser (2001) evolved his thinking and grounded theory, for example, by allowing for the possibility that the research is also entitled to define what is important and not only the study participants as posited, for example, in Glaser's study published in 1992. As an interim summary, the notion and assumptions of grounded theory versions evolved over time. Evans and Liverpool (2013) fittingly refer to the current state of the grounded theory approach as a maze, which can easily overwhelm a novice researcher first encountering it. Fernandez (2012) identifies starkly diverging four core approaches when reviewing the field critically: classic grounded theory or CGT (Glaser, 1978), the Straussian grounded theory by Strauss and Corbin (1990) emphasizing qualitative data analysis, the constructivist grounded theory

(Charmaz, 2000, 2006, 2014) and the feminist grounded theory (Wuest, 1995) enriching the field with a feminist perspective. Its focus on avoiding androcentric or male researchers' and research subjects' biases, along with an acknowledgement of women's voices in research communities, turn this approach more into a peripheral one.

Surely, gender issues can matter in building a dean-orientated leadership pipeline, as Davies (2015) indicates, and researchers will detect them in coding and categorising if a data analysis shows relevant insights emerging. This study, however, is not primarily a gender-difference-focused study. However, if similarities and differences across gender are not prioritised, voices from female deans could receive less consideration, which, in turn, impacts the creation of new insights and solutions.

When studying business schools' leadership pipelines, I adhere to a more modern, flexible approach as detailed by Charmaz (2014). Does this lead to an overdependence on one source or author although the analysis above draws parallels to fellow constructivist grounded theorists already? This can clearly be negated in line with Mills et al. (2006) clarifying in their review of constructivist grounded-theory-oriented authors that "without fail each of these authors/researchers drew on the work of Charmaz" (p. 31). Mills et al. (2006) establish that Charmaz's research provides guidance in the field: She "has emerged as the leading proponent of constructivist grounded theory" after previously being a student of Strauss and Glaser. Even Glaser (2007) labels her article as "excellent". Furthermore, Charmaz (2006, 2012, 2014) appears in juxtapositions of main grounded theory approaches as the scholar representing constructivist grounded theory (cf. Singh & Estefan, 2018). Following the mainstream of constructivist grounded theory helps learning from several of her publications on the method and an even bigger series of articles that apply her approach and which thus can serve as a source of inspiration.

While Charmaz (2006, 2012, 2014) counts as the originator of constructivist grounded theory, there are a number of additional researchers which have been elaborating and evolving the approach. This study equally draws on Tie et al.'s (2019) who elaborate on the role of the researcher's own lens when constructing, not discovering theory. They equally detail the coding process more and differentiate initial, intermediate and advanced coding. This finer distinction helps approach the coding process with more transparency and confidence about how to proceed in what Hoare et al. (2012) call the "dance with data" (p. 240) and what Breckenridge et al. (2012) describe as the co-construction of data. Tie et al. (2019) equally support a better understanding of the quality evaluation system, shedding light on what matters when critically reviewing a researcher's capabilities, a review of the fit between method and research question, and procedural precision. I simultaneously draw on Mills et al. (2006) explaining implications of constructivist grounded theory, in particular when it comes to carefulness when interviewing, memo-writing, constantly comparing, coding and integrating codes, and when structuring the interplay with the interviewees. This provides boundaries for the otherwise tremendously flexible approach.

As Shiobara (2018) outlines, constructivist grounded theory preserves the original logic of a comparative approach that Glaser and Strauss (1967) outline, while enhancing Corbin and Strauss' (1990) additions on structuring data for analysis as well as acknowledging a researcher's contribution to the process, such as the techniques of questioning and interpreting. Gaining these advantages comes at the natural cost of criticism. Glaser (2012) as one of the originators of grounded theory, attacked Charmaz (2006) complementing the grounded theory field with her constructivist view that the evolution of the field is a misnomer, as it should not be about latent patterns analysed situationally and constructively together with all of the interviewer's possible idiosyncrasies and biases.

Adherents of one school of thought on grounded theory, thus, cannot be too easily pleased or find acceptance from members of another subgroup within grounded theory researchers. Academics should consider accepting this, although it is not necessarily a new insight. Moses and Knutsen (2012) clarify that "for as long as can be recalled, we have argued over different ways of knowing. Gods, giants and even reasonable people cannot appear to agree about the nature of reality and how we can understand it" (p. 1).

Secondly, when shedding light on implementing a grounded theory project, Allan (2003) points to the lack of clarity regarding the coding process, which is central to grounded theory. He could not find a clear instruction on how to proceed, as neither Glaser and Strauss (1967) nor Glaser (1978, 1992) insist on or, more moderately, suggest one best manner or coding mechanism. Evans and Liverpool (2013) explain that "the process and methods for coding have created the highest level of debate for users of grounded theory" (p. 38). One option, the micro-coding of numerous individual words, can easily become time-consuming, confusing and lead to data overload. According to Allan (2003), the very manner in which researchers gather data matters substantially because interviews provide clarification, which might not be the case in other data collection methods, such as self-completed surveys. To address this challenge, Charmaz (2012) – complemented by the aforementioned researchers detailing the process – was used as guidance and interviews continued until theoretical sufficiency was reached. Previously, it was clarified that the sample size cannot be predetermined and as generalisation is not a goal of the study, the number of interviewees was deemed not necessarily bigger but sufficient. Interviewers should, however, receive training such that more of the interviews' true potential as a method materialises. I embarked on numerous exchanges with other grounded theorists and primarily reviewed the available literature in order to comply with Nagel et al.'s (2015) suggestion to ensure adequate skills are in place before proceeding with a grounded theory study.

The alternatives, – zooming out, – try to skip this step by simplifying and attempting to grasp the meaning, and the bigger picture risk violating grounded theory's underlying logic. After all, the constructed theory cannot stem from anywhere other than from it being grounded in data (Allan, 2009). Allan (2003) reports self-doubt about whether he is on the right track, something Charmaz (2014) suggests as part of the process, also in terms of saturation – the point in time when the researchers terminate analysis and interpretation. The author continues by outlining that publishing the results of a grounded theory can be challenging, as the ensuing comparison of data and the investigation of links can easily exceed the space assigned to a published paper. This is in contrast to publishing the results of a descriptive dataset and a regression analysis table, which might well need less space and, therefore, appear to be more complete and more transparent.

Thirdly, the quality criteria for grounded theory are rather comprehensive and include credibility, originality, resonance and usefulness (cf. Charmaz, 2005, 2006) – dimensions which other constructivist grounded theorists, such as Tie et al. (2019) mirror and detail. Chandrasegaran et al. (2017) likewise recommend visualisations during and also as an outcome of the theorising process. Section 5.5 addresses visualisations in light of the gained insights and theorising results. These various sets of factors are multidimensional and not free of subjectivity, thereby rendering critical evaluations of the quality of grounded-theory-based studies somewhat challenging. Carrying out a critical self-evaluation of the very manner in which the research question was addressed at this point means paying special attention to these criteria as guiding criteria in the ensuing analysis.

In sum, although Miller and Fredericks (1999) clarify that grounded theory has become the "paradigm of choice" (p. 538) for qualitative researchers, it is not an easy approach, as it places high demands on the researcher's skills, and requires transparency regarding the individual theorising steps. In the following Chapter 4, the results of the coding, categorising and category integration efforts ensue.

4. Emerging categories and constructed grounded theory

4.1. Introduction

This chapter presents the empirical results. The chapter has two main sections. The first part presents the emerging categories based on the process described in Chapter 3. They are each then discussed within the context of literature. These categories include the following:

- Non-linearity in section 4.2.

- Non-desirability in section 4.3.

- Non-specificity in section 4.4.

- Non-sequentialism in section 4.5.

- Non-existence in section 4.6.

The second part of this chapter shows the integrative grounded theory as an outcome of the data collection and subsequent abductive analysis in section 4.7. This abductive reasoning takes stock of observations through coding in order to draw conclusion through an iterative process of comparison and selective combination. What emerges, is a context-specific leadership development model for the role of dean based on what the participants in this study share.

4.2. First category: Non-linearity

Based on sample quotes and codes detailed in the following table, the interviewees helped generate a better understanding of the nature of the leadership-orientated career path in business schools. Discussions and quotes were coded. These codes led to an observation that the journey taken by those who are deans not necessarily lead to a deanship. I10 stated that "true stars don't have to be dean". I8 added that if someone really aspires to be a "knowledge guru", being appointed as a dean is not the greatest achievement. I12 underlined that "not many aim for a deanship". Then how did the candidates end up in this crucial role? It hardly appeared to be the result of long-term career planning. I1 clarified that "nobody aspires to be dean at a young age". I3 "drifted into it" without thinking about it a long time ago. Furthermore, also I9 admitted that the "deanship just happened like that". Similarly, I11 "somehow ended up in it". I4 concluded that "it is a career curse". I2 explained that it was not this drifting but fear that caused him to accept the call for duty – the fear that "a big idiot would do the job". The pattern remained the same: the deanship is not the core aspiration. Besides the deanship not being aspirational, it does not appear to be a position people remain in for long. I1 said that "the dean role is temporary". I4 clarified that "I am a serious teacher and that is not going to change". I15 was more blunt regarding the repercussions: "I will be a professor again soon and look forward to writing articles". Moreover, also I9 planned to return to teaching and research and I10 concurs that the dean role is temporary: "I have no plans to be a dean for long".

As an interim summary: In the business school context that was explored with these interviewees, it is not necessarily so that individuals remain at the level of a dean. Returning voluntarily to a role as professor, – be it to pick up a past role of researcher, teacher or both, – is not uncommon. Becoming a dean, is not a linear development for an organisation's top talent. It is likewise not a one-directional career path. Another element of non-linearity is that there are parallel tracks for becoming dean and remaining active after the deanship. Furthermore, the interviewees apparently care about being authentic over time. While they accept the role and its temporary nature, they would not want to compromise their authenticity in the long run. Being authentic and true to their main identity as faculty will cause the dean role to be a temporary one only. Career U-curves into the dean role might well happen, but so would a move out of it in the near future. This might well be linked to the second category, i.e. non-desirability, explored in the next section.

Table 2: Sample quotes and codes for the category of non-linearity

Interviewee	Comments	Codes	Category
I1	"Afterwards, I will do something to use the contacts, such as being in charge of acquisitions, but the dean role is temporary. Nobody aspires to be dean at a young age; that would be crazy".	Acknowledging that being dean is not a long-term dream	Non-linearity
I2	"I came from the corporate sector where I burned out …. Then I was a faculty member and I liked it a lot. I had freedom. Fear drove me; fear that a big idiot would do the job".	Making oneself aware of identity	
I3	"I drifted into it … I did not think about it eight to ten years ago".	Skipping long-term planning	
I4	"It is a career curse: I am a serious teacher and that is not going to change".	Aspiring to something else	
I6	"There are a lot of positions and it is not only one that means you self-actualise or rise up; for example, research, teaching, admin, selling …".	Being aware of the multitude of parallel career paths	

I7	"I started doing admin back in the day to evade the pressure to publish, but it was not planned at all; that would be too arrogant … and we are not that visionary here. Most people join for the academics".	Realising that leadership is less desirable than being an academic	
I8	"Being a dean is an administrative role; not a dream destination for someone with aspirations to be a knowledge guru".	Clarifying aspirations	
I9	"Deanship just happened like that. I will return to teaching and research".	Self-limiting and being authentic	
I10	"I was more of an entrepreneur turned faculty for entrepreneurship. I am still inherently an entrepreneur. I have no plans to be a dean for long …. True stars do not have to be dean".	Being self-aware	
I11	"I was a teacher and dealt with very different, unrelated topics. I somehow ended up as a dean".	Avoiding a structured career	
I12	"Leadership is not professionalised. Not many people have this goal".	Distilling the organisation's dominant logic	
I12	"It is more of a circular move; you return to where you are".	Coming back	
I13	"I was told again and again that I am a born leader; it was therefore clear that a leadership role would come, but just not the appointment as dean".	Remaining flexible	
I14	"I can only make a horizontal move to another dean role or maybe to a role with AACSB externally because, having stayed in the dean role for too long, I de facto lost my competitiveness as a professor".	Realising time limits	
I15	"I will be a professor again soon and look forward to writing articles".	Taking a U-turn	

4.3. Second category: Non-desirability

The interviewees stated quite openly that the role of dean is hardly desirable. They might have aspired after the power but soon realised it is a less influential role in reality. The following table sheds light on sample quotes, emerging codes and the overall assigned category. I5, for example, shares the following with I1: "I thought I had power, but they stopped me. So they want me to be dean, but not really". I1 shows similarities to the lack of control by stating "we are driven", but being dean is "still better than being a dentist". Advantages and motives for being dean would also not enable longer commitments. I4 clarifies that "for a woman, it is a good opportunity to make a difference but that effect wears off …. The salary differences are small too".

Therefore, if it is not power, role modelling or the financial incentive, what else can motivate a person to accept an appointment as dean? Interviewees appear to exhibit different drives and needs that run counter to remaining in the dean role. I8 expresses it quite bluntly by realising that "I moved away from what I wanted to do with my time" and I7 reiterates "I really want to teach", indicating a loss of being authentic, self-actualising and focused on what matters more. Being a dean is less glamorous, less fulfilling and overall less desirable than it should be for a more lasting role and responsibility. One of the factors that could aggravate the situation is the role's lack of specificity. The following section explores this further.

Table 3: Sample quotes codes for the category on non-desirability

Interviewees	Comments	Codes	Category
I1	"Okay, it is still better than being a dentist … but we are driven".	Being cynical	Non-desirability
I2	"They surely overpromised what I would be allowed to do".	Showing resignation	
I3	"As an academic, I want to be a balanced person with a balanced portfolio, including teaching and research … but now I have handcuffs and no power".	Missing balance and a rich portfolio	
I4	"For a woman, it is a good opportunity to make a difference, but that effect wears off …. The salary differences are small too".	A lack of lasting motivation and incentives	
I6	"Too many hearts beat in my chest; this is not sustainable. And if you do not publish, you are left out of the academic community".	Sacrificing too much	
I7	"I really want to teach."	Not being authentic	
I8	"I did not want it. I like research, but when I did the MBA, they noticed my abilities. I moved away from what I wanted to do with my time".	Not self-actualising	
I9	"It is not so desirable; too much admin".	Understanding the job better	

I10	"The dean is no longer viewed as a professor; it is them against you. People also feel sympathetic towards the dean".	Breaking the bond	
I11	"You do not volunteer for the dean role …. It is not a very intellectual role at all …. The norm is to be faculty again …. You have to be careful if you were too strong a dean, because then your peers might reject you later on".	Starting to feel repulsion	
I12	"I was a professor, I am a professor and I will be a professor afterwards".	Being true to oneself	
I13	"I wish I had more entrepreneurial freedom, but (the school's) owners restrict me".	Feeling limited	
I14	"Being a dean means you are done as a researcher. You lost touch".	Perceiving the risks	
I15	"I thought I had power, but they stopped me. They want me to be dean, but not really".	Giving up	

4.4. Third category: Non-specificity

Discussing the actual dean role yielded the following results. As exemplified with quotes, codes and the emerging category in the following table, 1) the dean role is not homogenously specified across business schools, 2) it may similarly not be pre-specified, 3) the dean role appears to vary drastically from a larger to a very limited scope of responsibilities and 4) there are diverging interpretations depending on the situation.

For example and referring to 1), I4 suggests that international benchmarking may not hold universally: "We started with a profile from the US but then did what we thought would be required. I do not do fundraising". Situational set-ups diverge. I8 adds an interesting insight when elaborating that the status and organisational goals can account for different roles. I8 states that "we are somewhat different, as profit does not matter; we optimise quality". With reference to 2), I2 clarifies this quite aptly by sharing that "there was no charter or job description …" and even if there is a job description, it may well not be implemented as planned. In this context, I7 illustrates just how much non-compliance there was: "They planned exactly the opposite of what I do now [interviewee laughs]". With reference to 3), the scope of the role appears to be vast, ranging from a presidency-level major and rich interpretation to being a rubber stamp (I10), exemplifying a reductionist view whereby the dean merely signs off invoices without much opportunity for comment (I15) and merely do "as told" (I5). Lastly and addressing feature 4), the interviewees share that they observe different success factors, be it "silver hair" (I1) and, thus, seniority or mere potential (I9) and pragmatism (I3). In contrast to these success factors, other interviewees emphasize harder factors, such as networking (I4) or student proximity and business acumen, even if it means weaknesses on governance or accreditation expertise (I3), a focus on entrepreneurial skills and priorities (I6) or cultural sensitivity (I12).

Considering the ambiguity of what the role prescribes, the extent to which expectations are binding, the degree to which skill expectations are standardisable and the level of discretion allowed to interpret the role freely with a unique focus, it can be difficult to prepare well and meet expectations. This includes personal expectations as well as contextual ones. Furthermore, if the career steps in business schools are not sequential, it might not be easy to accumulate skills. This is the focus of the next sections.

Table 4: Sample quotes and codes for the category on non-specificity

Interviewees	Comments	Codes	Category
I1	"You need silver hair to be accepted".	Viewing seniority as key	
I2	"There was no charter or job description …. The university president liked my pragmatic skills; I never had a role model".	Noticing the vagueness of the role	
I3	"I have always been fond of students and good with business, not governance or accreditations".	Emphasizing selected strengths	
I4	"We started with a profile from the US, but then did what we thought is required. I do not do fundraising".	Diverging from plans	
I5	"I never intended to be dean. I am dedicated to the university and I regarded deanship as rendering a service. Therefore, I do as I'm told".	Subordinating	Non-specificity
I6	"I interpret it as an entrepreneurial role".	Underlining and prioritising entrepreneurship	
I7	"They planned exactly the opposite of what I do now [interviewee laughs]".	Choosing freely to bring the role to life	
I8	"We are somewhat different, as profit does not matter; we optimise quality".	Understanding the need to have an idiosyncratic set-up	
I9	"They must have seen potential; that is it".	Focusing on mere potential	

I10	"As soon as they appoint you, they control you without room to breathe …. In fact, now I am just a rubber-stamp administrator".	Reducing the role to a narrow, complying one	
I12	"You need to know the national culture; you cannot simply lead with a yes or a no. A lot takes place informally".	Contextualising the role	
I13	"We classify the role more as one of presidency and, thus, as a more senior role like classic deans".	Enlarging the role	
I14	"I am a network manager; I invest in networks. That is it".	Prioritising networks	
I15	"It is admin, nothing more … similar to an executive director role, but academically I have little to say …".	Limiting the role	

4.5. Fourth category: Non-sequentialism

Sequentialism in leadership tracks refers to the career feature that foresees a noticeable continual enlargement of responsibilities ranging from leading oneself, leading smaller and then larger teams through to leading a unit and those who are team leaders – and possibly leading across units or even entire entities as part of a group. Similarly, non-sequentialism refers to the phenomenon that a skill needs to be used to prevent atrophy. It cannot be built up too early without practising due to the risk of atrophy. Certain ideas and solutions also have a shelf life before they become outdated. Prioritisation also plays a role. If something is not needed right away, it would be more worthwhile to focus on other skills. New tasks require new skills, which, in turn, necessitate unlearning.

Quotes, codes and these two categories, i.e. sequentialism and non-stocking, were eventually combined into one as part of the focused coding process, as the overlap was substantial. There were dominant quotes and codes as discovered during the constant comparison. The following table details samples, illustrative quotes and codes along with the overall emerging combined category. Previously reviewing the literature, – at least as it was done preliminarily, – supported the spotting and labelling of a number of sub-phenomena.

Table 4: Sample quotes and codes for the category on non-sequentialism

Interviewees	Comments	Codes	Category
I1	"Nobody starts on a clear leadership track".	Lacking long-term views	

I1	"First of all, it is a business; we need specialists in different roles".	Emphasizing specialists over leaders	
I2	"The president has little ambition … only a few years left …. He does not understand what is required".	Clarifying the role of the structure versus the agent	
I2	"The first dean was a professor, tenured and an endowed chair … could not use any skills then".	Comprehending the lack of transferability of skills	
I3	"I somehow ended up in executive education and admin".	Going with the flow instead of steering	
I4	"Being a teacher and doing research does not help at all, if at all; colleagues notice that I have stopped filling my publication pipeline".	Acknowledging group values and pressures	
I4	"I never learnt how the university really works".	Noticing gaps	
I5	"I did learn how to lead the grad school business, but this is different".	Understanding gaps	Non-sequentialism
I6	"In firms, you have power at the top, in B-schools only trouble; where do you learn leadership skills?"	Spotting insufficiencies	
I6	"Research skills do not help you lead".	Comprehending the fragmentation of skills	
I7	"I have seen the world, gained consulting experience as well as a doctorate, but with that I could have gained a position anywhere else".	Playing an active role as agent	
I8	"It is almost impossible to prepare".	Adopting a fatalistic stance	
I8	"You have to be an academic to qualify and become socially accepted, but this is different from learning the skills to lead".	Realising discrepancies	
I10	"I have built insight on sustainability which I cannot use now".	Understanding sunk costs and unlearning needs	
I11	"Professors have their specialities: It is not leadership".	Acknowledging limitations	

I11	"Academic experience is irrelevant if you have to lead".	Valuing skills in relation to tasks	
I12	"You have to have published, but that is different".	Perceiving incompatibilities	
I13	"It is most important to see eye to eye with the owner (of the school), but that can change fast; being competent then matters less".	Enlarging the relevant set of competencies	
I13	"It has nothing to do with planning and therefore you cannot prepare".	Perceiving limits to plannability	
I14	"I was a vice-dean, but that does not really help, as the roles are different".	Delineating limitations	
I14	"You have to accept blind spots and ambiguity, and work on it then and there".	Embracing uncertainty	
I15	"I was never head of department or vice-dean. It was a big jump. Probably too big a jump, I have to admit."	Realising the need to grow gradually	

The lack of sequentialism starts with a lack of awareness of what is needed. This could be due to the organisational leaders not being ambitious enough. This was illustrated by I2, for example, when stating that the institution's presidency is close to retirement and stopped bothering: "The president has little ambition … and has only a few years left …. He does not understand what is required". This can then boil down to an emphasis on operations and not an emphasis of the organisation's transformation over time. I2 shares that "first of all, it is a business; we need a specialist in their roles". Specialists in the role of dean are, like professors, surely required. "Nobody starts on a clear leadership track" said I1, thereby showing what a specialist in the role means for leadership development.

It is, therefore, not surprising if people merely move around in organisations without a clear, strategic pursuit of talent acquisition and allocation. In order to illustrate this, I3 shares the following: "I somehow ended up in executive education and admin". I4 points to the lack of strategic learning about how the organisation operates, – an essential aspect of leadership development for future transformational leaders, – by revealing that "I never learnt how the university really works". I6 then asks the justified question, i.e. when to learn the skills required to lead: "In firms you have power at the top, in B-schools only trouble; where do you learn leadership skills?"

Yet, skills, even if they are excellent, lack relevance for subsequent leadership duties as interviewees made clear. This applies especially to professors. I2 confirms that his previous dean could not apply his experiences as a tenured professor. I4 posits that "being a teacher and doing research does not help at all, if at all; colleagues notice that I stop filling my publication pipeline". I6 continues by outlining the same shortcoming: "Research skills do not help you lead". I11, in turn, exhibits similar levels of self-awareness by taking a clear position on the following: "Professors have their specialities: It is not leadership". The risk, therefore, is that promotions to the dean role represent too much of an overwhelming step. I15 admits in this context that "I was never head of department or vice-dean. It was a big jump. Probably too big a jump, I have to admit". A number of previous experiences are simply irrelevant. I1 similarly states: "I was a vice-dean, but that does not really help, as the roles are different".

This likewise applies to content-level expertise as I10 admits: "I built up a lot of insights on sustainability, which I cannot use now". I6 summarises it aptly when he says that "research skills do not help you lead". Just how far apart content expertise is from beneficial acumen, I13 puts in words when paraphrasing experiences: "It is most important to see eye to eye with the owner, but that can change fast; being competent then matters less". Such a stretch of skills and linked learning or unlearning must help interpret I8's conclusion that "it is almost impossible to prepare".

What lacks, are opportunities to accumulate knowledge and skills, which have been better thought through. More integrated plans might possibly help in this regard. But do such plans exist? The following section reviews experiences by the interviewees.

4.6. Fifth category: Non-existence

One of the key experiences elicited during the interviews focused on the extent to which the study participants perceive detailed, effective leadership pipelines or, for that matter, any kind of structured, structure-induced development efforts on which the aspiring dean candidate can rely for his or her development. The following table, – as the table before, – shares sample quotes, codes and the emerging category of non-existence of such leadership pipelines in business schools in the explored settings of the study participants.

This study revealed that in the study participants' organisations there is a gap between holistic, proactive, long-term leadership developments in line with the leadership pipeline concept known from the corporate sector and the leadership pipeline concept as described in the literature review section. Five main reasons account for this obvious gap between what the literature suggests should be in place and what the interviewees experience. Firstly, there might be a lack of awareness. I2 shared: "There is no pipeline in place. The big boy is not aware of the need".

This might well have been facilitated by the second reason: an external supply of candidates trained by other institutions – and with their training paid for by someone else. I3 clarified that recruitment could take place from a global source of applicants: "There is always someone available out there .... The expat pool is big … and it discourages a longer time for self-development". By a significant contrast, I7 appears to work for a purportedly luckier organisation with noteworthy amounts of top talents. I7 states that "we have so much talent, there is no need to structure something". This is clearly the exception, as most interviewees appear to implicitly or explicitly agree with I14 who states that "it is learning on the job and you have to accept this. There was no systematic approach; there is an undersupply of deans".

Table 5: Sample quotes and codes for the category on non-existence

Interviewees	Comments	Codes	Category
I1	"It is more difficult in business schools to form leaders, as the pipeline is initially filled with different talents …. They do research or teach, sell or administer".	Realising skills gaps	
I2	"There is no pipeline in place. The big boy is not aware of the need".	Identifying a weakness	
I2	"Fear was the final straw; they would have promoted an idiot otherwise".	Competing motives	
I3	"There is not much grooming in here … talent management is simply not done".	Wishing for more leadership development	
I3	"There is always someone available out there …. The expat pool is big … and it discourages a longer time for self-development".	Relying on external recruits	
I4	"They just do not want to; it costs too much money".	Prioritising cost	Non-existence
I6	"There is no talent management; we do not walk the talk".	Not walking the talk	
I7	"We have so much talent, there is no need to structure something".	Working with an abundance of talent	
I7	"Since I have ambitions, I prepared myself to 80% but remained a generalist".	Taking initiative as an agent	
I8	"I had to become more of an extrovert; nobody told me to".	Embarking on personal development	
I9	"It is more spontaneous".	Realising the emergent nature	
I9	"There is no development journey; you only attend to the actual things required".	Optimising situationally	

I10	"It had to be someone from the outside, as there is no internal programme. It would involve too much cost and create too many expectations. What do you do if you upskilled three candidates?"	Being critical	
I11	"There is no programme and on the job it might be too late; I did the EFMD mini-course for deans myself, but that was too short."	Understanding the need for development	
I12	"It is learning on the job, as things had to go very quickly ... people decide for you on what to do, the system dominates ... but this does not mean the same for learning as well".	Being driven	
I13	"I never had a leadership role or team responsibility, but I did request coaching".	Becoming active at low levels	
I14	"It is learning on the job and you have to accept this. There was no systematic approach; there is an undersupply of deans".	Acknowledging demand and supply	
I15	"Interestingly, they pushed me into this role but gave me no training"	Lacking holistic thinking	

The third reason might relate not to the external supply but the cost of growing internal talent. I10 clarifies this by positing that "it had to be someone from the outside, as there is no internal programme. It would create too much cost and expectations. What do you do if you upskilled three candidates?" This leads to risk factors attached to the cost – a leadership pipeline would mean several candidates have expectations and this could cause frustration if someone is not chosen.

Fourthly, the interviewees shared that these leadership pipelines are simply absent. I3 says that there is "not much grooming in here ... talent management is simply not done". Professionalisation of talent management has not reached business schools. This might also lead to more pragmatic initiatives from the school's side and, as I9 says, "It is more spontaneous". I12 explains that the timeframes for selection and onboarding were rather short, necessitating more spontaneity. The experiences were "it is learning on the job, as things had to go very quickly ... people decide for you on what to do, the system dominates ... but this does not mean the same for learning as well". I9 argues similarly by stating that "there is no development journey; you only attend to the actual things required".

Fifthly, there appears to be substantial passivity among candidates as the purported agents in their structure. I15 reveals major passivity when criticising the institutions: "Interestingly, they pushed me into this role but gave me no training". If there were proactive agent-driven initiatives, they were minor only. I13 admits, "I never had a leadership role or team responsibility, but I did ask for coaching". I11, in turn, went on a training programme for deans: "There is no programme and on the job it might be too late; I did the EFMD mini-course for deans myself, but that was too short". An outlier case is I7 as mentioned before. The interviewee works in an organisation that has a lot of leadership and did not consider it necessary for the organisation to put together a structured programme in light of this abundance of candidates. Interestingly enough, I7 thereby triggered more proactivity, apparently to avoid falling behind in a competitive setting: "Since I have ambitions, I readied myself to 80% but remained a generalist". Somewhat in line with I7 taking charge, is I8 who revealed that "I had to become more of an extrovert; nobody told me to". Leadership pipelines do not exist in the business schools represented in this study, due to these starkly varying reasons. There are a few additional observations learnt from the interviewees, which are highlighted in the next section.

Additional observations on learning on the job

One of the key experiences elicited during the interviews focused on the extent to which this study aimed to explore how the interviewees perceive the phenomenon of a potential leadership pipeline. In the course of the interviews, the study participants also shared substantial learning on the job. I1, for example, realised "I learned how to be authentic and not only being driven, but driving .... I learnt that alumni have networks and I learnt how to tap into this". I2 "practiced mindfulness, learnt to slow down and get the rhythm right". I3 revealed the following: "I evolved naturally in the position, learnt how to communicate, to move forward in spite of hurdles and to understand the local context better … I took a previous dean as a mentor". I3 admitted "I learnt pragmatism and still do what I want, such as mentoring a few doctoral students". I5 revealed to have "… learnt how to reinterpret and implement my dedication, – my altruism, – differently".

I6, in turn, realised the following: "I studied politics; now I learnt how to do it". I7 admitted that it was impossible to rely on help or take a mentor as "… that would mean I am weak; I now work on my character to be a role model". I8 understood the need for situational leadership: "As the role is changing and the environment too, you need to learn how to be effective situationally". In contrast, I10 took a mentor. Furthermore, I12 understood the Darwinist forces at play by sharing that "recruitment was first slow, then very fast; I had to professionalise my leadership to survive". The time available to then grow in order to merely stay in the dean role for a shorter period of time appears to be tremendously short.

4.7. Integration of categories and emerging grounded theory on leadership-oriented ship canals

The following figure depicts the grounded theory that emerges as a result of this empirical study. As leadership development represents a process that unfolds over time, it is not surprising that the horizontal dimension and x-axis in this explanatory visualisation perpetuate this time dimension. The vertical y-axis adds to the analysis of the leadership-acumen level, which can range from being rather limited to extensive. Leadership acumen in this context refers to sound judgement on strategic leadership decisions and behaviours. It includes both a sharp intellect as well as effective instincts.

Figure 4: Visualisation of the emerging grounded theory of a leadership-oriented ship canal for dean development in business schools

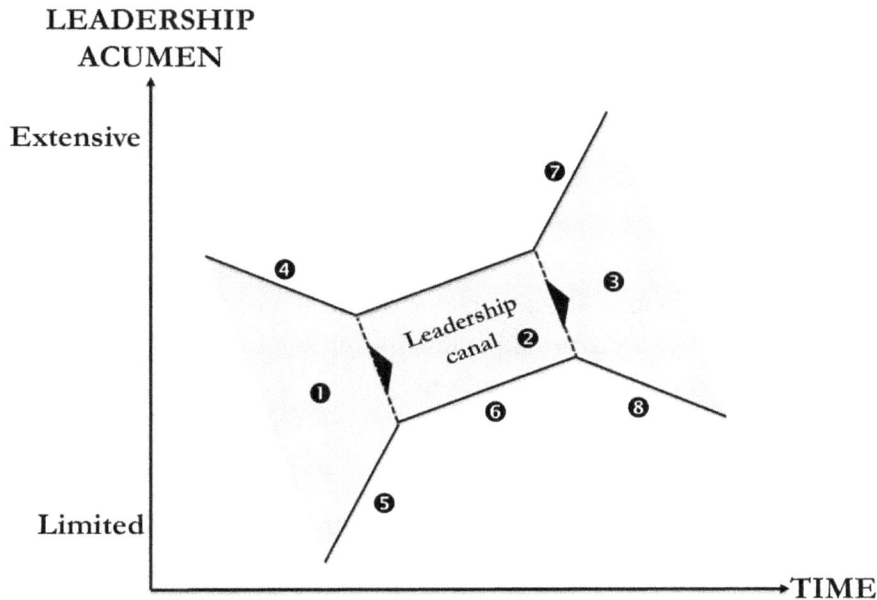

These two dimensions, i.e. leadership acumen and time, span the frame for the proposed grounded theory's true core, which builds on a new analogy along with a different label for the dean-role-leadership-development phenomenon as perceived by the interviewed deans. A guiding analogy can capture a framework's essence.

This study proposes to relabel leadership pipelines into leadership-oriented ship canals, aiming to depict and understand the phenomenon of leadership development in business schools as represented in this study more adequately. No further claims for generalisations are made. A ship canal refers to a connection between two large bodies of water (for a more in-depth review of technical aspects of canals, cf. Luebbecke et al., 2014). Transferring the analogy to leadership development, the figure above with its numbering of key features helps the explanation, yet the preceding analysis, quotes, codes, categories and memos serve as foundation for this emerging framework. The pipeline analogy no longer applies, as it refers to a much longer timeframe candidates spend in it from being a member of a team right after graduation and joining the corporate sector, up until becoming a group executive often three, four or as many as five decades later. Relying on semantics, commencing with "non" further emphasise the stark differences between a leadership pipeline and a leadership-oriented ship canal, and what would usually be expected in a non-academic corporate context.

Zone 1 refers to the first body of water (the pre-canal zone or pool of talents), which would feed into the leadership-oriented ship canal. This pool is big, as internal candidates as well as a vast pool of external candidates (possibly recruited globally) are available. Internal candidates could comprise talents with extremely low levels of leadership competencies. This is exemplified by the canal's wide opening and the delimitation line 5. Visually, it is a steep line alluding to the steep learning curve they would still have to cope with and which can happen quite rapidly with little time for compiling an onboarding plan. An interviewee mentioned coaching, another candidate attending an EFMD seminar for deans, both of which are rather limited interventions.

Delineation line 4 marks the other side of the pool of talents – the other side of zone 1 that feeds into the canal. Individuals with substantial experience from other sectors, such as being an accomplished entrepreneur, could also feed into the canal. These kinds of individuals would require unlearning, as leadership in a smaller or medium-sized company would not necessarily be easily comparable to leading an academic institution with tenured professors and established pay structures. Even being a vice-dean would hone a number of leadership skills, but the level of complexity and the tasks shift once the person is promoted to the deanship, which requires recalibration and unlearning.

Then follows the leadership-oriented ship canal – zone 2 on the figure above. Timewise, it is a shorter zone, as individuals appear to pass through it rather quickly. Number 6 similarly indicates that the interviewed candidates learn on the job. They either learn how the institution really works or learn how to use networks, thereby becoming more extrovert, developing the acumen to manage relationships with the owners, running different teams, becoming highly pragmatic and revisiting emotional intelligence because there appears to be a situation characterised by power games and other sources of frustration, such as being reduced to mere administrative roles. Individuals miss teaching and research. Zone 2 as the true leadership-oriented ship canal has clear delineation lines at the beginning on the left-hand side and also at its end on the right-hand side. These delineation lines allude to the arguments on non-specificity and non-stockability. Past experience might not be as useful entering the true leadership-oriented ship canal, with the same logic applying to the post-canal zone.

Zone 3 depicts the aspired zone (the post-canal zone) that many aspire to more than staying in the dean role. Learning on leadership could of course continue, for example, by adopting not only institutional responsibilities but an industry-wide one as I14 pointed to when outlining the option of working for the industry association AACSB. Their learning in the field of leadership could therefore continue to grow as depicted by delineation line 7. In contrast, the majority of interviewees shared that they prefer to return to being a professor and avoid the career curse of being a dean. This would not require these specialised leadership skills. They might well atrophy over time as depicted by the downward slope of delineation line 8.

4.8. Discussion of the emerging grounded theory with extant literature

There are several elements of the leadership-oriented ship canal for business school deans that are distinct. They are reflected in the categories identified above and will be discussed with additional literature in the following. Therefore, the subsequent linking of the constructed grounded theory to extant literature continues to reflect the theoretical sensitivity (Strauss and Corbin, 1990) I as the researcher built up after the preliminary literature review and theorising grounded in the collected data. This theoretical sensitivity continues to serve the purpose of separating "the pertinent from that which isn't" (Strauss & Corbin, 1990, p. 44). Although this study follows the example provided by Charmaz (2012), also Strauss and Corbin (1990) emphasise the need to grant centre stage position to the story. Thus, the ensuing sections zoom in on the core categories identified above, clustering in pairs if it furthers the juxtaposition with the extant literature.

Firstly, linear versus non-linear career paths emerge as a truly essential feature of the leadership-oriented-ship-canal theory in light of the non-linearity (see section 4.2) and non-sequentialism categories (see section 4.5) detailed above. The section below reviews this insight in light of the extant literature.

Secondly, and exploring the non-desirability and non-specificity categories portrayed in sections 4.3. and 4.4 further, there is literature that helps interpret findings further. Specifically, two streams appear to be relevant: The underlying leadership philosophy in terms of being a transactional, transformational or transcendental leader represents the first body of knowledge in the extant literature. This stream addresses the servant leadership type of orientation interviewees portray. From a sociological point of view and as discussed below, this adds structural stability. This argument is very much in line with insights gained from the preliminary literature review, which foresees a rather fuzzy or situational role profile for the business school dean. Adding criticality to the analysis, identity theory can add perspectives, which help interpret the empirical findings. Do deans merely pretend to sacrifice substantially to pre-empt criticism and build a more tolerant environment? The section below discusses insights from identity theory research.

The third literature-related section below deals with the non-sequentialism category identified above in section 4.5. Accelerated, just-in-time and just-in-need learning must result from a much shorter timeframe for the incoming deans' preparation and onboarding periods. Lastly, the fourth section deals with the non-existence category previously outlined in section 4.6. Self-regulated learning and personality styles become obvious as core trait of these canals. Based on the aforementioned absence. Together, the following sections critically discuss all key features of the leadership-oriented ship canal and deepen the understanding of the constructed grounded theory in line with the research objectives.

Exploring non-linear professional career development

Oliver et al. (2020) recently revealed for the UK that only 15% of business school deans move on to higher positions, 25% make a lateral move to a similar position elsewhere, 25% retire but the biggest segment of 35% return to being a professor. This pattern supports this study's finding on non-linearity. It also corresponds to the ship-canal analogy, with the post-dean phase seeing all kinds of options. Practitioners, such as Agarwal (2018), acknowledge the existence, relevance and even benefits of non-linear career paths. The academic literature as part of the stream on career theory embraces non-linearity in careers as outlined, for example, by Sullivan and Baruch (2009). The authors present alternatives to the linear, systematic, one-way upward mobility as either a desirable or a feasible model. According to them, they view older linear models as dated, because they describe too much of a stable organisational environment and extrinsic incentive systems as key motives for a drive upwards in hierarchies. Developing beyond this linear model is the Protean career pattern proposed by Hall (1996) which offered substantially more flexibility, raising the importance of learning and emphasising the role of intrinsic motivation. Subsequently, Briscoe and Hall (2006) envisaged an individual possibly being more self-directed and values-orientated.

There is a link between study participants, their self-directedness and acknowledging essential building blocks of careers. Sullivan and Baruch (2009) juxtapose these two more modern concepts with boundaryless careers (Arthur & Rousseau, 1996). Here, individuals could be portfolio-orientated and deliver services to more than one employer, which is of less relevance to this study, as deans, in their roles as figureheads, can represent one organisation only.

Furthermore, there are further variants, such as Peiperl and Baruch's (1997) post-corporate careers. This variant has a certain relevance to the study, as one participant was an entrepreneur before, viewing a business school as a post-action, a less intense challenge. Greenhaus et al. (2008) underline the multidirectional nature of careers. Super (1957) differentiates between careerist types and inter-organization mobility for a more aggressive version. This connects to the experiences shared in this study, i.e. external supply and outside talent pools for deans globally. The repercussion might well be a reduced effort in organisations themselves, not developing next-generation dean talents, as the market for it appears to be efficient. Otherwise, the schools or the ambitious candidate carry the cost if there are only insufficient investments in leadership development.

To conclude, an interesting analogy for careers stems from Mainiero and Sullivan (2005). They argue that individuals base their career decisions on three points – authenticity, balance and challenge. The interviewed deans appear to renounce authenticity and seem to compromise what inspires and drives them. As indicated, theoretical triangulation caused a bit of ambiguity on whether the renunciation of authenticity is active impression management and, thus, an outright lie or not. However, if the interviewees were truthful, they would have renounced authenticity, being true to themselves and their values.

The multifaceted nature of authenticity can render the analysis quite complex, as Van Leeuwen (2001) states that there are elements of being genuine or a light is shed on all the complex social processes of establishing authority and integrity. Such details are less relevant at this point. More important is the divergence of the career-theory variant put forward by Mainiero and Sullivan (2005). Not only do the interviewed deans sacrifice, they sacrifice their research or teaching desires; the clear majority also renounce authenticity in general by being micromanaged and subordinated. The deans' balance appears to be off, leading to short tenures and high turnover. Deans aspire to catch up with other activities dear to them. The motif of challenge does not necessarily apply either. Deans, to a certain extent, do as they are told; they comply and if there is any truth in the impression management argument – or accusation – then they fight an impossible challenge with manoeuvres.

The challenge factors as the third construct in Mainiero and Sullivan's (2005) model also comes in the form of what, for example, Kompanje (2018) labels burnout and compassion fatigue, not merely burnout risk. Bruch and Menges (2010) outline how such energy losses can drastically impact performance. This applies to those who are perceived as being too reductionist, playing a rubber stamp role during their dean tenure. This is relevant, because if the insight spreads that the dean role is too boring for a specific organisation, any motivation to prepare extensively fades. There are opportunity costs as well, which come in the form of distractions from publishing efforts or keeping one's thought leadership.

There are three distinct observations when reviewing the literature in light of the produced grounded theory. Firstly, the idealist, almost romantic view of a leadership pipeline lacks the integration into the larger set of theories on careers. Granted, leadership career theories might have a different, narrower focus than the more generalist career theories critically reviewed by, for example, Sullivan and Baruch (2009). The insights on non-linear careers should also be more present in the pipeline-orientated models.

Secondly, this insight applies even more in the specific context of business schools where professors represent the core pool of talent to recruit from. Thirdly, there are aspects that emerge from the data in the study that cannot be holistically and fully explained by either the leadership pipeline models or one or, for that matter, all of the aforementioned selected career models.

Contradictions are stark at times. In the research by Mainiero and Sullivan (2005), the gap between the model's assertions and the observations expressed by interviewed deans could not be more extreme. The established career theory models simply do not fit and there is a need for a new model, such as the proposed leadership-oriented ship canal.

Leadership philosophy, structural stability and identity theory

The preliminary literature reviewed in section 2.5 refers to definitions and various waves of leadership philosophies over time. The preliminary literature review concluded that a modern approach to leadership might possibly have three foci. The first one emphasizes the role of leadership versatility. Based on Kaplan and Kaiser (2003), the most effective leaders are versatile. This train of thought applies to leadership development (in this case the leadership-oriented ship canal) as well as the tasks of a dean – and especially their tasks' lack of clarity based on the **non-specificity argument** laid out above in accordance with the interviewees' experiences.

The next, more modern approach rendered Western's (2013) currently dominating eco-leadership phase relevant to this study. Deans ought to create convinced followers and positively impact the system. More specifically, Kim and Mauborgne's (2014) blue ocean concept applies to the extent to which, for example, owners or alumni must be convinced to perpetuate their support. Thirdly, Hodgson and White's (2001) recommendation that leaders must be learners also strongly applies to the leadership-oriented-ship-canal idea based on the interviewees' comments.

When it comes to the detected leadership behaviour shared by the interviewees, several observations can be made. Hodgson and White's (2001) suggestion that leaders are learners continues to apply. The deans need to adjust quickly. Therefore, within the leaders-are-learners view, it appears reasonable to specify the importance of learning agility (Lombardo & Eichinger, 2000) more than the importance of mere general learning. The onboarding and the time in the canal are short. Moreover, after leaving the leadership-oriented ship canal, there are fundamental shifts. Therefore, learning agility, – including its sub-constructs of mental, people, change and results agility, – cannot be overemphasized. Ideally, candidates either bring along a more innate learning agility or development efforts are made, either by the individual or the organisation, to hone it.

Moreover, based on the experiences shared by the interviewees in this study, the leadership-oriented ship canal shows links to the leadership-type trilogy of transactional versus transformational versus transcendental leadership (see Gardner, 1990). Transactional leaders set goals and milestones, measure progress with key performance indicators and, after controlling for results, issue the reward or mete out the punishment. Transformational leaders still implement plans and tasks but improve organisations in the process.

Transcendental leaders mirror true servant leadership (Greenleaf, 1970) based on altruism even to the point where the interests of others are prioritised over the leader's interests, and the leader's needs are sometimes completely excluded from the factors that matter. A number of interviewees viewed themselves as mere administrators, heavily controlled in their reduced space. What dominates their experience, however, is that they subordinate their needs to what the organisation and its governing bodies impose on the individual. The interviewees' experiences do not venture into spirituality as part of transcendental leadership as portrayed, for example, by Chumbley (2019).

What the interviewees point out, also does not relate to what Kezar and Holcombe (2017) call shared leadership in the context of higher education. The deans in this study appear to temporarily accept that their transcendent leadership primarily benefits their institutions. Rost (1991) defined leadership from an exchange-theory viewpoint as "an influence relationship among leaders and followers who intend real changes that reflect their mutual purposes" (p. 102). The interviewees in this study, however, appear to subordinate and sacrifice their personal needs or purposes. The interviewees are clearly more contribution-focused as foreseen within a more selfless transcendental leadership. Furthermore, leadership is not defined in a partnership as suggested by Cordoba (2000). Actual exchange relationships matter less. Overall, the interviewed deans are far removed from the hubris phenomenon as stated by Owen and Davidson (2009).

These authors reveal that an individual's charisma, his or her charm and ability to effectively deploy inspiration, persuasion, vision, risk-taking and self-confidence are, when linked to leadership, deemed a success. Unfortunately, however, this link also has downsides, such as hubris in the form of too much pride, overconfidence or even contempt for colleagues. In light of their selfless orientation, the interviewed deans stand in stark contrast to deans that exhibit such hubris.

The last section underlines the interviewed deans' contribution to the overall organisation of a business school. The applied perspective is leadership and, thus, a core business view. Adding a sociological perspective to the second literature review, Henslin et al. (2015) map the three dominant theoretical perspectives: structural functionalism, symbolic interactionism and conflict theory. The last section referred to a strong theme emerging from the discussions with them, mirroring a structuralist-functionalist perspective.

Dew (2014) explains this perspective further in that it highlights how an individual's action helps create stability for the business school as an entity. The underlying assumption is that there is a need for solidarity and cohesion. Deans indicate a clear social order and the dean's role is a more passive one. This also requires conformity and certain degrees of role conflict as well as ambiguity, possibly even overload. Role ambiguity can, for example, show in Posner (2009) labelling deans as pracademics, since they pursue practice-orientated and academic credibility. The conceptual counterpart is symbolic interactionism. This concept focuses less on the question of why there is and should be social order on a rather macro level, but more on how meaning emerges within dynamic networks of interacting parties on a micro level. These networks have less normative social pressure, and individuals do negotiate. Conflict theory emphasizing the struggle for limited resources is excluded from the analysis due to less relevance in light of the interviews.

The interviewed deans themselves share their perspectives. They reveal, to a certain extent, their views on the macro level. Goffman (1958) adds a useful analogy for analysis. He differentiates between prescribed roles, which are very much in line with structural-functionalism, versus more improvised, emerging ones, which are in line with social-interactionism. The interviewed deans appear to play rather prescribed roles and comply with expectations – with the consequence that the overall order in the organisation is not disturbed.

Each individual has to play a role. The aforementioned selflessness whereby roles are interpreted relatively passively regarding leadership development for deans, indicates an experience that fits well and clearly within the structural-functionalist approach. None of the probing as part of the theoretical sampling outlined in section 4.4. points to an alternative truth or a need for a contrasting theoretical view – if the developed grounded theory on a leadership-oriented ship canal remains solely grounded in data.

This section's purpose, however, is to discuss the empirical findings in the context of the extant literature, aiming to enhance the critical review as well as improve the understanding of the model. A somewhat contrasting interpretation becomes possible when linking the findings to insights posited by Brown et al. (2019) for business school deans and leaders in other sectors (Maclean et al., 2012). Their analysis deals with business school deans, advancing stark claims that these deans might not really be that selfless after all. Their research is relevant for understanding the empirical efforts carried out in this research project. Brown et al. (2019) suggest that business school deans use a purported loss of research or teaching opportunities as a resource within manoeuvres to create their identities. Apparently, emphasizing and perpetuating their loss and sacrificing their narratives lower the risk for them. Deans are viewed as active in a game of impression management. This might possibly mean there are downsides to this communication strategy as well, such as losing an image of being an excellent teacher or thought leader in research. The authors conclude their study by stating "it is perhaps the industry requirement for deans to wed themselves (unrealistically?) to demanding requirements that they author themselves as research-credible, moral and hardworking that in part accounts for their high rate of turnover" (Brown et al., 2019, p. 18). Moreover, since deans sacrifice so much, a demanding environment might well be more lenient. These authors present a dark view on deans. They might well be manipulative, deceiving, self-serving, displaying strong self-interest by not cutting ties with fellow academics in light of espoused values and even self-harming to anticipate and counter criticism.

Next to Brown et al. (2019) portraying business school deans as potentially rather smart communicators, Thomas and Davies (2005) find similar efforts towards crafting identities in business schools. It is a coping mechanism for their role conflict as Shumate and Fulk (2014) reason for the context of higher education in more general terms. Billot (2010) and Dann et al. (2019) clarify how central identity as a concept is for individuals working in higher education. Maclean et al. (2012) share that Chief Executive Officers in companies behave similarly when actively shaping their identity for their context. Van Maanen (1979) even warn of deliberate misinformation and also Langley and Meziani (2020) reckon that this proactive and pre-emptive "identity work" (p. 381) usually has at least a partial fictional nature.

However, the empirical study presented in Chapter 4 is not a discourse analysis. None of the probing in the later interviews appeared to indicate that the deans fake answers. This could, of course, not rule out a perpetuation of games and impression management even when deans perform outside their organisation and in a confidential setting from which they might perceive fear. Both Athens (1994) and, before him, Goffman (1963) assume such action to occur when interacting with others but explicitly also in soliloquy, i.e. when being by themselves and disregarding any audience there might be – similar to an actor in a theatre. Deans might well show a preference for being consistent in their narrative. However, only further research can clarify this question.

Accelerated, just-in-time and just-in-need learning needs

One of the leadership-oriented ship canal 's features is that the time frame for learning before and during the deanship might be very short. Time for onboarding can be seriously limited to the short term and deans' limited tenures do not allow a longer period of honing skills. While CEOs' tenure appears to become longer, even topping eight years according to Dixon (2016), a dean's average tenure is dropping to significantly less than eight years with only a minority of more deans staying on longer (Davis, 2014).

The question arises as to how far the model's assumption of accelerated learning or just-in-time learning represent new insights and can be connected to the established literature. The concept of leadership pipelines traditionally involves individuals staying a minimum of time in each stage to prove themselves, for example, by producing the right results and showing the desired behaviours, mature in the stage and overall qualify for the next levels.

The literature on learning embraces the two related phenomena in the form of accelerated learning, – which applies in principle to the time right before becoming dean as well as the time during which the individual functions as a dean, – and just-in-time learning. Hence, theory would not challenge the feasibility of an accelerated formation period with an intense just-in-time acquisition of what is needed. In this sense, there are strong parallels between the learning behaviour abstracted from the interviewees and the adult learner in more generic terms (Knowles et al., 2011).

The adult learner's readiness to learn becomes geared towards the social roles to play. Learning needs to be immediately applicable, not stockable for a potential point in time in the future when it might become useful. Killi and Morrison (2015) outline the changing learning requirements and move beyond the just-in-time learning to add just-in-need learning. The authors emphasize the importance of frustration as a driver for learning, which could be a useful perspective for the interviewees.

Learning can then occur neither too early nor too late, i.e. after the dean's tenure is about to end or has ended. The authors similarly point to "pressures to complete" (Killi & Morrison, 2015, p. 757). Thus, a shorter tenure for deans could also be interpreted as accelerating their learning.

There are multiple definitions for this acceleration of learning. Imel (2002) views acceleration of learning as a multidimensional design with the learner truly being placed in the centre of the learning. Already back in 1996, Schornack (1996) coins the notion of acceleration as 1) bringing about earlier, 2) increasing the speed of and 3) hastening a regular process or 4) enabling a learning of more in a reduced time frame. Thereby, the definition of relevance is mostly 2) and 4), – not 3), – in terms of an undue hastening or 1) in the sense of preponing, as this neither complies with observations gathered from the interviewees nor with the logic of the leadership-oriented ship canal.

This logic could apply in a very straightforward manner, as there would only be one individual in the dean-formation process or a maximum of a few candidates being groomed, which is in contrast to often heterogeneous class participants in business school degree programmes, to name only one example. In turn, Boyd (2007) posits that acceleration refers more to the very format in which learning takes place. Firstly, acceleration breaks free from traditional, pre-set and imposed periods and relies on a different approach for life-long learning. Bradner (1996) argues similarly and critically scrutinises the very approaches that are available for acceleration.

Bruch and Menges (2010) add that acceleration is a coping mechanism for an ever-changing world, and learning to prioritise and focus when in such a situation helps individuals survive. Beal (2007) outlines that experience in life, reaching a certain age, multitasking, – which is what the deans need to do maintain a minimum level of research or continue teaching irregularly, – perform rather well during accelerated learning. Wlodkowski (2003) warns of certain downsides of accelerated learning but overall confirms it to be a growing trend.

Moon et al. (2005) point to the crucial role technology plays in accelerated learning efforts. For Jao (2014), it is not necessarily technology. Senior leaders would, according to him, benefit most from working with mentors if they wish to accelerate their learning. Since several deans who participate in the empirical study outlined in Chapter 4 admit to working with mentors, there is a congruence of the leadership-oriented ship canal with this previously published recommendation.

As an interim summary: Accelerated learning has been explored in the literature (Boyd, 2007; Bradner, 1996; Imel, 2002; Schornack, 1996; Wlodkowski, 2003). While there is a certain amount of criticism that accelerated learning comes at a cost, such as superficiality, the academic literature acknowledges the three essential elements of desirability, feasibility and opportunity, for example, in terms of omnipresent technology.

Self-regulated learning and personality styles

Research objective 2 asked how the leadership development responsibilities are perceived to be divided between schools and candidates for the dean position. Based on the **non-existence argument** presented in Chapter 4, this research project revealed that there is generally no consistent, holistic, proactive and long-term system in place.

Yet, as the following figure illustrates, there must be an explanation for the observed phenomenon that, regardless of what the organisation as the overarching structure does for the individual as the an agent within it, any individual with aspirations has the freedom to proactively prepare for future roles or remain passive. Reviewing the literature, two possible explanations emerge for this phenomenon. The one explanation stems from personality profiles and the other from a self-regulated learning view. As for Kabele (2010) pointing to the split of responsibilities as a sociological view on what the organisation versus the individual ought to do, the following figure maps behaviours observed in the empirical study presented in Chapter 4.

At the same time, this figure also illustrates that Kabele's (2010) split of responsibilities might well be a too simplistic an explanation. As will be made evident, it does not naturally follow that if the organisation does not assume responsibility for leadership development, the individual would automatically do so and repair the damage. Due to a lack of an open dialogue on this responsibility and other priorities, – such as teaching, research or a focus on administrative tasks as shared by the interviewees, – leadership development fails to be an explicit priority. Yet, how does one explain that a number of individuals still broke the norm and asked for coaching, thus revealing potential weaknesses? How does one explain that a few individuals consciously chose to attend an EFMD seminar, – by their own choice, – and shared with peers that this was done to emphasize readiness? How does one account for other deans represented in this study who organised mentoring?

One relevant explanation stems from adding the personality trait perspective to this discussion. Vaught et al. (1989), for example, represent an early start to this train of thought. These authors transfer an insight from leadership to the educational sector and review how personality traits impact administrators' behaviour, including their communication behaviour. Vaught et al. (1989) rely on the psychometric test, the FIRO-B tool (Fundamental Interpersonal Relationship Orientation – Behaviour). As outlined in the following figure, the tool explains behaviour with the help of individual scores along three dimensions – the extent to which an individual wants to include others, wants to control what is happening and relies on any form of external affirmation or affection.

Figure 5: Categorisation of individual learning behaviour observed in the empirical study – in relation to the business school's efforts

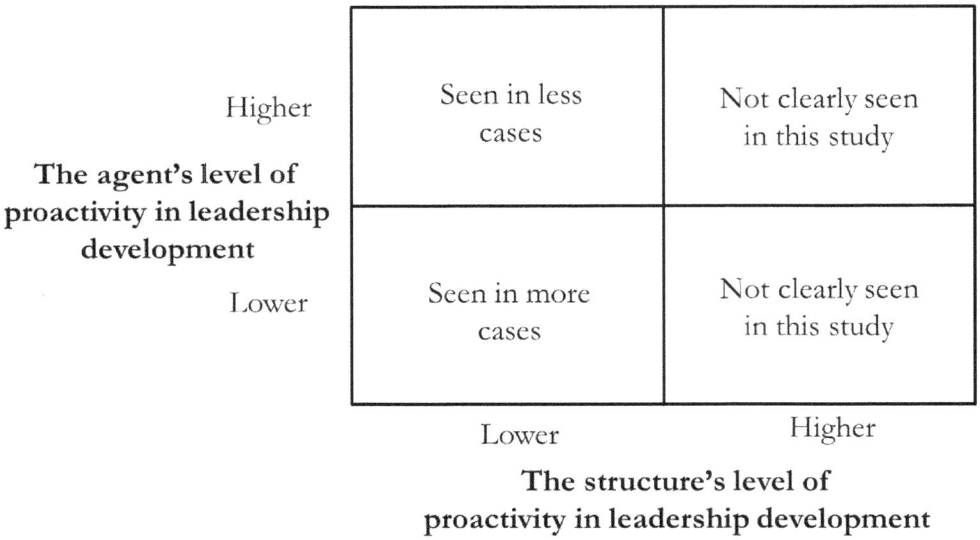

Higher	Seen in less cases	Not clearly seen in this study
Lower	Seen in more cases	Not clearly seen in this study

The agent's level of proactivity in leadership development

Lower   Higher

The structure's level of proactivity in leadership development

Before continuing with the application of the FIRO-B as a tool, a brief evaluation is needed in line with the aforementioned considerations on thinking styles. the tool's underlying three-dimensional theory for interpersonal relationships and behaviour emphasizing inclusion, control and affection was originally published by Schultz (1958) who posits that people would always need other people – yet the degree to which this is true for an individual varies starkly. Krause et al. (2008) as well as Fleenor and Van Velsor (1993) are positive about the instrument and provide validation.

Exploring the theory and tool further, there are more critical voices. Hurley (1992) questions the tool's internal reliability but also the fundamental idea of assessing interpersonal behaviour with mere intrapersonal measurement. DiMarco et al. (1975) criticise the lack of interdependence amongst the three dimensions and conceptual overlap. Salminen (1988) points to social desirability issues. Over time, not only more psychometric weakness but also doubts about interpersonal compatibility prescriptions emerged while the tool continued to be in use as, for example, Macrosson and Semple (2016) exemplify. In spite of these acknowledged shortcomings, Furnham (2008) clarifies that the theory and measurement tool with its 54-item questionnaire enjoy ongoing popularity amongst management consultants and organisational psychologists, although this is not the case amongst academic psychometricians and personality theory experts due to a degree of obscurity. In the following context, the tool is not used for a statistical analysis, nor is it presented as a cutting-edge operationalisation of interpersonal behaviour and compatibility per se. Relying on the tool in the following, resides in its popularity amongst practitioners as outlined by Furnham (2008) and its usefulness when sensitising for problematic areas. Furthermore, in line with Grau (2019) and when characterising an individual's preference for including others in their development, for sharing control and for seeking affection from others, the instrument provides a pragmatic orientation.

Figure 6: Basic FIRO-B dimension to explain human behaviour

	Inclusion/ involvement	Control/ influence	Affection/ connection
Expressed	Expressed inclusion	Expressed control	Expressed affection
Wanted	Wanted inclusion	Wanted Control	Wanted affection
	Sum I	Sum C	Sum A

Source: Based on Schutz (1978)

Higher affection scores can also translate into fear of breaking bonds, for example, by demanding too much. The model differentiates between what an individual wants from others and how the individual would, in turn, treat others, which is less relevant in the perspective of a next-generation dean.

Linked to this view but still complementing the analysis, is the field of self-regulated learning, which Pintrich (1995) regards as a field of great importance. Boekaerts (1991) details several objectives that foster self-regulated learning. These objectives can include general curiosity and an interest in learning, minimising harm and threats and living up to commitments. Irvine (2019) enriches this train of thought by juxtaposing older and newer learning taxonomies in his critical review of how individuals learn. He clarifies that more recent contributions go beyond self-regulation as part of the metacognitive system and embrace a self-system. Here, as Marzano and Kendall (2007) argue, a learner makes a crucial personal choice at the very beginning of a learning process. The learner scrutinises the importance of what needs to be learned and concludes whether it is worth the effort. Furthermore, this analysis includes considerations of whether the learner has the self-efficacy to go the distance with possible learning efforts. This, in turn, requires a review of the ability to sustain motivation and how to best respond to learning challenges.

The study at hand shows strong desires among the interviewees to not become irrelevant as a researcher. They share their perception of sacrificing their desire and strengths to be active as a regular faculty, be it in the field of teaching or research or in other fields. Based on this train of thought, dean candidates should embark more proactively on more self-drive leadership development. Dean candidates should turn into more active agents in the aforementioned structure versus agency debate. They ought to take a clearer stance in the debates about who drives the leadership development journeys and who ensures that sufficient leadership skills will be available when needed. Future studies ought to conceptualise and operationalise these constructs for subsequent empirical validation.

4.9. Summary of the differences between a traditional leadership pipeline and the emerging leadership-oriented ship canal for business school deans

This chapter dealt with a second literature review – an eclectic one aimed at critically reviewing how to better understand the emerging grounded theory of a leadership-oriented ship canal compared to insights in the extant academic literature. The following table aims to summarise converging and diverging factors. Based on the aforementioned empirical and critical literature analysis, it becomes obvious that a leadership-oriented ship canal differs fundamentally from leadership pipelines. While a leadership-oriented ship canal foresees a much shorter period to develop the leader, leadership pipelines might well apply in the non-academic corporate sector. There, more investments into longer-term development journeys for internal candidates and clearer role during and at the end of the development dominate. There are clear leadership tracks in the non-academic corporate sector where the survival of the fittest produces candidates to occupy positions, possibly rotating horizontally, but without taking career U-turns to lower levels, as career tracks are assumed to be linear.

Table 6: Summary of the comparison of this study's context-specific leadership-oriented ship canal in business schools versus a general leadership pipeline

Criteria	Leadership-oriented ship canal	Leadership pipeline
Assumption about existence of desired career goal	Deanship not a career goal	Executive position as the final target for the fittest
Role and competency clarity	Deanship is ambiguous	Executive position quite clear
Time frame for development	Very short term	Long term, even multi-decade at times
Role of learning on the job	Essential	Important, but only a part of an overall holistic formation journey
Perceived discretion of incumbent	Limited	Broader
Assumption about quiddity of learner in nature versus nurture debate	Nurturing (in an accelerated manner) is emphasized	Nurturing (over decades) is emphasized
Exchange relationship	Deans focus on selfless contributions	More pronounced exchange relationships with executives pursuing own agendas

Overall maturity of the field	Only this study at hand available	Multiple pipelines exist
Assumption of linearity of careers	Not assumed, deans are open to U-turns	Assumed to apply to the fittest candidates
Universality claim	Not made, leadership-oriented ship canal thus far only applies to the study at hand	Universality and cross-sectional validity assumed
Assumption about cost-benefits of candidate development	Often disadvantageous, as external markets are efficient and tenures short	While external markets might well be efficient, heavy investment cost observed
Tenure period	Rather short with high turnover	Longer periods desirable, but observing a shortening as well
Possibility of games being played	Not observed in study, but in literature on deans	Observed in theory and practice

Leaders in non-academic corporations would then wield more power than the often tightly controlled deans in their reductionist roles doubting if they even have any existential significance, which can account for their role fatigue (Kompanje, 2018). As this table illustrates, a new gestalt, – a new variant of model, – emerges from the produced theoretical framework that is based on the grounded theory. The subsequent Chapter 6 provides gained lessons and a critical review of the research process, before Chapter 7 outlines implications and Chapter 8 concludes this study.

5. Implications

5.1. Introduction

Chapter 5 continues implications for the leadership development of deans both from a theory or research point of view as well as practice. More precisely, section 5.2 provides high-level implications for the field of leadership development in general. Section 5.3 elaborates on the implications of this research on leadership development in business schools. Section 5.4 continues by breaking down implications to the level of individuals who might aspire to becoming a dean. Simultaneously, these sections follow a structure of key knowledge and learning areas originally found in Aristotelian semantics and critically reviewed by Millo and Schinckus (2016). The framework depicted below differentiates a set of notions based on where they can be positioned in a matrix in which a theory versus practice as well as a knowledge versus wisdom continuum is considered. The idea, thereby, is to move beyond what the Greek referred to as mere *daxo* – a quite simple, unsubstantiated opinion on a topic.

Figure 7: Overview of knowledge-related constructs

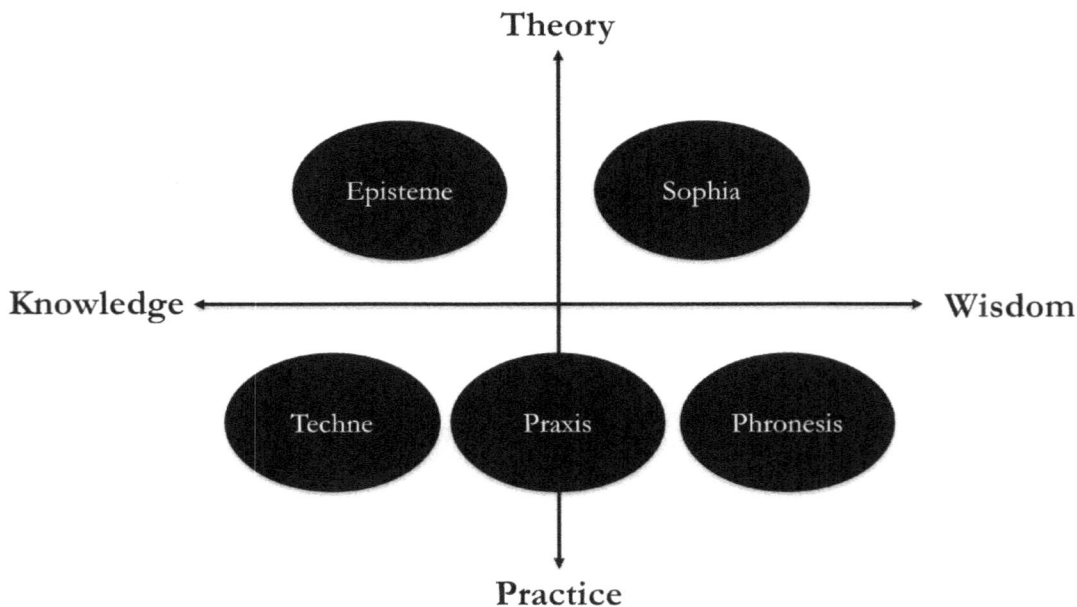

Source: Based on Millo and Schinckus (2016)

As visualised in this figure, techne addresses very practical knowledge and related skills, while episteme focuses more on the quiddity or nature of a construct from a more theoretical perspective. Praxis moves beyond techne to focus on more abstract principles with which the techne ought to be handled. However, the principle level foresees special cases and exceptions. In turn, the phronesis addresses practical wisdom while sophia addresses the wisdom on theorising, including the research process. These semantics categorise the outlined implications.

5.2. Implications for theory on leadership development in general

As outlined in the figure above, episteme deals with the theoretical nature of constructs. There is one main implication for the field of leadership and its development in general. Earlier, this research clarified that Glaser and Strauss (1967) distinguish between two types of theories. A substantive theory is context-specific. Its alternative in the form of a formal theory becomes generic. This research project presents a new substantive theory in the form of the leadership-oriented ship canal reflecting the perceptions of the interviewees.

This distinction can be linked to the field of leadership in more general terms. The produced grounded theory in the form of the leadership-oriented ship canal for business school deans serves as the foundation for the argument that the field of leadership might well have made great progress when it comes to breadth due to its search for generic, more universally valid models. Blue ocean leadership (Kim and Mauborgne, 2014) is presented as a panacea-type, integrative, general model. McCauley (2020), in turn, presents a more simplistic tri-partite leadership model emphasizing direction, alignment and commitment (ADC) with the claim of universal validity as well. However, formally, too generic concepts, such as blue ocean leadership and its core reliance on market logics, ADC with its reductionist view on three tasks only or the aforementioned leadership pipeline, can inspire vertical enrichment of the leadership and leadership development fields – and conceptual depth require substantive, i.e. context-specific, models as well. They might inspire context-specific reasoning and solutions, contributing to relevance. The suggestion moving forward is, thus, to further encourage additional efforts in what Western (2013) labels as eco-leadership – a very context-orientated lens on leadership. As outlined in the following figure, leadership has a considerable breadth of insights across sectors, industries and organisational settings, indicated by the horizontal bar of the capital letter T.

Figure 8: Breadth versus contextual depth in the field of leadership development

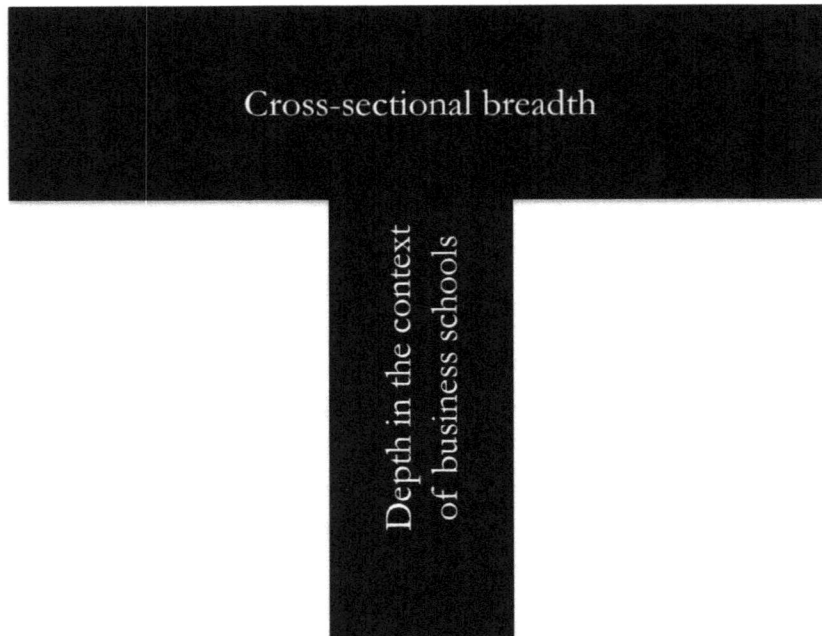

This T would only be complete with a vertical, context-specific part, which ensures enough substance that is specific to an individual context. While no claim to generalisation is made when it comes to the leadership-oriented ship canal, this grounded theory indicates the importance and relevance of a specific setting. Examples from other more diverse and context-specific areas could be leadership (development) issues in churches (Tamunomiebi et al., 2018), criminal organisations, such as the mafia (Catino, 2014), government organisations (Ingraham & Getha-Taylor, 2004) and student bodies (Rosch & Collins, 2017). Adding an international lens, spotting a specific setting's inherent patterns in several countries could indicate the need for more research efforts along this train of thought.

5.3. Implications for leadership development in the specific context of business schools

Zooming in on this specific context, the following question arises: How could and should one improve practice in the real-life business school setting? The ensuing suggestions can best be characterised as praxis, – as principles for further professionalisation, – instead of its two alternatives: techne or phronesis. Techne would prescribe detailed steps, possibly for each of the 15 participating deans and their schools.

In contrast, suggestions on the phronesis level would yield clear practical wisdom; however, without further empirical testing or taking very context-specific factors on the organisational as well as the personal level into consideration, suggestions on the phronesis level would be an overly ambitious goal for the still-early stage of development studies on deans in business schools.

Therefore, on the praxis level, the proposed model of the leadership-oriented ship canal primarily serves the purpose of exploring and understanding how participants experience the phenomenon of leadership development. The interviewees commented on their personal situation along with practices in their current institutions. They indicate suboptimalities, which show in the following forms.

Institutions risk a hastened preparation instead of a more long-term approach to build required stakeholder management, organisational change or communication skills more thoroughly, to name but a few examples. There could be unnecessary excess frustration instead of a more conducive self-actualisation. There is a risk of sacrificing authenticity at the cost of satisfaction for having achieved yet another career step. There is a risk of too short a tenure to really act as an effective transformational leader. In addition, more and more schools rely on other institutions taking over the formation of next generation deans, believing in efficient markets, yet thereby creating frustration. Aspiring leaders would not enjoy resources and experience leadership opportunities, which would be allocated if a real pipeline concept was in place. Schools want to recruit experienced candidates but none is willing to help a candidate grow as a leader. This creates suboptimalities for the entirety of schools. In the long run, this can cause a shortage of available leadership talents. Exploring the professionalization of how deans are readied can adopt the institutional view and a system-wide perspective across individual schools.

As this research initiative focuses on the experiences of selected interviewees, there are suggestions for their contexts. Starting with a review of a business school's responsibilities, two levels matter. The first level is each organisation's commitment to organisational excellence and role modelling as prescribed by the PRME addendum principle. The second level then explores governance. The following sections elaborate on both.

Bringing the PRME addendum principle to life

All the interviewees work for PRME member schools that have committed to the addendum principle. This principle calls for the PRME business schools to become authentic, impressive and ever-improving role models, not merely publishing or teaching about how other individuals or institutions ought to behave. Efforts towards the addendum principle should (and usually can) be increased. However, a business school does not have to be a member and commit to the fees or reporting obligations in order to work towards improving the status quo. Member organisations are simply obliged, but there is space for more voluntary innovations amongst non-members as well.

Godemann et al. (2014) stated that only "little attention [had been] paid to the addendum/additional principle" (p. 20). Role modelling can involve noticing that not enough leaders are produced – neither for one's own institution nor for others. Role modelling would also lead to a stronger realisation that publication or teaching excellence might well be qualifier skills for next-level assignments but are unrelated to what leadership skills must be portrayed later on. Instead of perpetuating suboptimalities and logical gaps, next generation solutions are produced. Implementing this could be done in the form of a leadership talent pool with a minimum of resources or acknowledging and assessing leadership effectiveness or versatility as part of recruitment, retention, promotion and remuneration policies or mentoring programmes. The PRME encourage organisations to be role models, to walk the talk — raising the question, why should a business school merely teach or research on how to develop leaders but not adopt best practices itself? If it does, it can only enhance credibility and the quality of its leadership.

This train of thought can be linked with the specific context of an institution. *Figure 1*Section 2.3 as part of the literature review differentiates four types of institutions based on their prioritisation of organisational versus scholarly impact as dimension 1 and teaching versus research priorities as dimension 2. Leadership development programmes that are more holistic and longer term can mirror the organisation's position. In a social science institution heavily focused on scholarly impact via research, transformational and transcendental leadership qualities could focus on evolving the research effectiveness in a noteworthy manner. The transcendental nature of the relevant skills could then once more be linked to responsible research as part of the PRME. In stark contrast, Ivory et al. (2006) also foresee self-styled professional schools. These schools pursue actual organisational impact via teaching rather than rigorous research for top journal publications. Aspiring high-potential leaders could be identified with an eye on transforming programmes over time, motivating and coaching faculty to reach peak performance or improving crisis management skills when managing students. Alignment of organisational logic and the focus of leadership development are key.

The same logic applies when linking this section's insights to the second model of seven strategic groups of business schools outlined in the literature review. This framework put forward by Iniguez de Onzono (2011) can equally help apply the lessons learnt. Leadership development in a local provider versus a globally integrated school logically differs drastically. The more diverse the served markets abroad are and the more the internal integration should yield synergies, the more the complexity skills matter in such a transnational organisation (Harzing, 2000). In local schools as per the framework, which operate in a locally or regionally more isolated space, success logics differ fundamentally as Ghemawat (2011) details. Stakeholder management in locally complying manners, abilities to impact businesses or society locally and local fundraising could form part of such context-specific tailored leadership development programmes.

It goes without saying that the other variants of organisations portrayed in section 2.3 of the literature review call for their own idiosyncratic features when it comes to identifying and developing next generation leadership talents in an effort to avoid the shortcomings of the ship canal presented in Chapter 4. In principle, this logic does not have to be limited to business schools. It can apply to other institutions of higher education or organisations in other fields where leadership development efforts are equally underdeveloped. A case in point could be a non-profit organisation with limited resources, which has hitherto relied on efficient labour markets to tap into talent pools.

As for the employer organisation where I currently work – equally located in effective external labour markets – the non-existence of leadership development efforts should be overcome with local organisational leaders, the personnel department or the dean of faculty introducing rather common career-planning efforts at the headquarters' level. As a globally active, integrated market leader in line with Iniguez de Onzono's (2011) typology, there is ongoing and growing demand for leaders and high performance beyond the classroom or research activities. The cost of headhunters could be offset at least partly with commencing internal development initiatives. There is an expected positive impact on the attraction, retention and further motivation of talents, as more career and personal career opportunities render the employer more attractive. After clarifying responsibilities of business schools, the ensuing section continues with deliberations on governance.

Clarifying governance

The second level is to clarify governance and it addresses the question of who is in charge of ameliorating current approaches to leadership development. This could be the board, president, CEO, chancellor, vice-chancellor, executive director, executive committee, senate or a chief human resource officer. Deciding on a topic champion can unfold in several manners to reflect the diversity of schools. Yet, the responsibilities must be clearly allocated.

Then, there is a need to focus on self-awareness and the possibility that leadership development can be a construction site – an area of sub-optimality. A process of gathering updated data on pending challenges and demands for leaders must ensue. Taking this initiative forward, it can be revealing to explore if a business schools faces major challenges with the dean. Institutions may well vary regarding efforts in forming the candidates for deans internally. Some institutions may well have carried out explicit cost-benefit analyses to determine whether recruiting externally, e.g. via headhunting, versus developing own talent can be more beneficial. Such cost-benefit analyses comply with the optimisation-orientation so common in business school research and classrooms. Another important factor to consider is whether the institution envisages radical or incremental change. External candidates with relevant experience can enrich and complement the internal set of capabilities and talents. In addition, organisational energies matter. The deanship can cause frustration. The individual who holds the position can disengage and the same logic applies for followers.

Subsequently, organisational leaders and decision-making entities, such as senates or boards, take a fundamental decision between make or buy, or a hybrid approach, i.e. preferably sourcing talent from outside the school versus developing them internally. Similarly, a fundamental decision ought to be made regarding the organisational approach: systematic versus emergent.

Certain organisational cultures in business schools could be highly bureaucratic on one end of the continuum versus rather organic and autopoietic. This has to acknowledge a business school's individuality, based on the organisational history, the vision and mission, idiosyncratic goal systems, the organisational culture, resources, level of political games, etc.

Next, institutions could foresee a risk-mitigating anticipation of potential reasons why the chosen approach would not work. A business school that is about to lose its independence or is about to take over another organisation could quickly render decisions outdated. A consideration is to ensure that organisational members and key stakeholders have a shared understanding of the subsequent improvement process. Based on these initial steps, the aforementioned entity should then set the course for the leadership development strategy within the larger organisational governance. Lastly, it is about acceleration and continuous improvement. Each organisation is different, with a unique overall strategy and business model. Each one pursues their specific objectives, mission and vision, organisational culture and resource endowments, and their governance bodies must bear the responsibility to decide how fast and in how many directions they should evolve.

It is important to ensure that these overarching boundaries are aligned with the leadership development strategy. Section 2.3 detailed main business-school gestalts, which provided a useful orientation. The following figure clarifies what this boils down to. Based on the systematic versus organic approach and a fundamental decision in favour of primarily a make or buy option, there are repercussions for the leadership-oriented ship canal. The following figure differentiates four main scenarios, which are detailed in the following. The resulting 2x2 matrix can serve practitioners as a point of orientation and reflection on their own setting.

The more systematic and make-orientated a business school aspires to be, the bigger the shift from dominating pragmatism, short-termism and conscious or latent acceptance of substantial risk has to be, since leaders for dean roles might not be as well-prepared as they could be, referring to the interviewees' observations in this study. This might impact their tenure negatively, which lowers their potential to have impact. If a school opts to perpetuate the status quo, the leadership-oriented ship canal is likely to persist. The concept will be less needed, – similar to a pipeline, – the more a business school decides to recruit externally and outsource leadership development to other schools.

Figure 9: Approaches to securing leadership talent in business schools

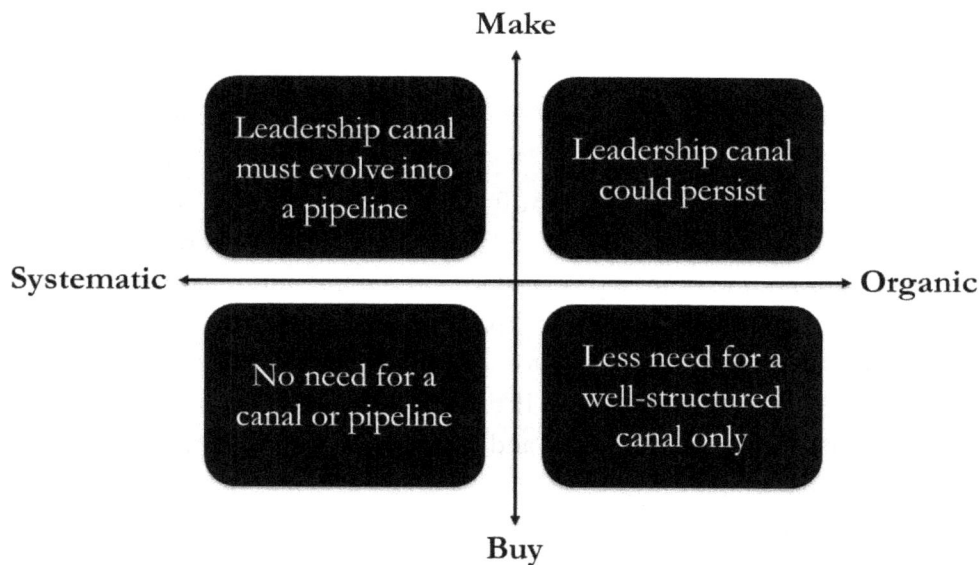

Make

> Leadership canal must evolve into a pipeline

> Leadership canal could persist

Systematic ← → **Organic**

> No need for a canal or pipeline

> Less need for a well-structured canal only

Buy

This train of thought can be linked to the suggestion that as part of a holistically applied addendum-principle philosophy, a culture of constant and never-ending improvements should be fostered even more, which includes the dean role and which is regularly reported on in the PRME reports. On a level below the global United Nations Sustainable Development Goals and PRME initiatives, there are regional or country-based initiatives to encourage innovation and quality throughout institutions. Fisher and Tallant (2015), for example, analysed the Teaching Excellence Framework (TEF) and the Research Excellence Framework (REF) for the UK. Business schools can indeed benefit from these external impulses.

Business schools might, however, possibly benefit even more from a relevant, next-generation Governance and Leadership Excellence Framework (GLEF) taking into account the local contexts. The goal must be to move the dean role from a frequent weakness to a clearer strength based on truly making the role work for all – the institution as well as the incumbent. This argument can also be considered in terms of the four-frame model originally proposed by Bolman and Deal (1991). The authors reveal that one can understand organisations by viewing them from a structural, a human resource, a symbolic and a political viewpoint. Therefore, perceiving organisations, which include business schools, from a political viewpoint has a long tradition. Politically active groups or individuals, pursuing at times conflicting interests and diverging levels of skills, priorities and resources for playing political games can then lead to rather suboptimal settings.

Thus, it should not surprise if reality then diverges from this call for clearer roles and the call for turning the dean role into a strength and an assignment that works for more parties. Politics can cause this idea to derail and fail. Further empirical testing of the generated insights can help generalise these insights for a wider group of business schools.

5.4. Implications for practice from the view of aspiring next-generation dean candidates

The first implication is that candidates must clarify their values, identity and career aspirations. What is the candidate's personal vision? Does the candidate value teaching, research or other impact? Does the candidate aspire to be an academic or pracademic? Does the candidate aspire to become a thought leader in applied research or rigorous, scientific discovery? Or does the candidate aspire to be a senior leader and is there a corresponding readiness to not only build teaching and research skills so as to enable credibility but also leadership acumen? If the structure and the employer would not organise and pay for it, is someone ready to screen and fund leadership initiatives in addition to other responsibilities and workloads? These are crucial reflection questions.

In my work context, I took a decision to launch this research project to further qualify for additional responsibilities, thereby compensating for a lack of structure-provided training opportunities. Even before COVID-19, organisational busyness did not enable much room for leadership development initiatives. At times, the agent has to prioritise. Thereby, the research project at hand still enables synergies. The agent's prioritisation catalyses learning directly from the literature, from the interviewees, from the grounded theory that had been developed, considering all personally relevant lenses while simultaneously creating research that can be submitted to conferences, journals and book publishers. This research and learning effort complements attending leadership seminars provided, for example, by the European Foundation for Management Development (EFMD) and its Strategic Leadership Program for Deans[1], which solely focus on practical skills.

Forray et al. (2015) illustrate the unique potential of the Principles of Responsible Management Education (PRME) initiative. This initiative can also address the issue of a lack of clarity regarding the dean role. Based on this logic, becoming a dean requires honing transformational and transcendental leadership skills, ensuring the right ethical imprinting on oneself and the organisations. This renders the skill set already one step more concrete. Role and value clarity can pre-empt criticisms on deans as put forward by Brown et al. (2019).

This analysis originally started with pointing to the Red Queen effect characterising the business school industry. Iñiguez de Onzoño and Carmona (2012) detail that achieving true, sustainable competitive advantage is difficult, as, according to this Red Queen effect, business schools need to

---

[1] https://www.efmdglobal.org/learning-networking/professional-development/strategic-leadership-prog ramme-for-deans/

change to merely survive. As soon as they have changed, more evolutions or revolutions of practices become necessary.

Suggesting to the next generation of aspiring candidates what to do, must therefore include leadership versatility as outlined by Kaplan and Kaiser (2003), as each situation – and each ever-changing situation – is different. Aspiring candidates ought to likewise hone their just-in-time, just-in-need learning on the job and their learning versatility, i.e. learning in a variety of modes, such as in preparatory seminars, with the EFMD, coaching or mentoring.

Candidates have to reflect upon and grow their learning agility. Lombardo and Eichinger (2000) list related constructs when elaborating on this learning agility, which can include mental agility, people agility as well as change and results agility. This substantially exceeds the capabilities individuals usually build up that enable them to qualify for positions and promotions in business schools. In this context, Tovstiga (2015) distinguishes between what is needed to play versus what is needed to win. Research, teaching as well as administrative and sales skills represent skills needed to play in a business school, to be hired and promoted.

In a faculty-driven institution, the emphasis shifts to academic factors. However, academic factors are a detour when it comes to building up the skills needed to win: transformational, even truly transcendental, leadership and versatile, agile learning skills.

This boils down to substantive extra efforts in a personal leadership development journey for which, – at least this is what the interviewees in this study report shared, – there is little to no organisational support from the surrounding structure in which these agents act. This requires resources in terms of time, energy and money.

Therefore, – and this is something that the leadership-oriented ship canal can learn from its counterpart, the leadership pipeline, – the aspiring next-generation candidate must have really deliberated well what the career goal is and then embark on a more long-term development, which the leadership-oriented ship canal describes as practice, albeit a flawed practice.

Identity (Brown et al., 2019) and blue ocean thinking (Kim & Mauborgne, 2014) are constructs that were discussed in the second literature review. The interviewees in this study had identity issues. Serious candidates for dean roles have to operate a blue ocean logic, as they compete for different reasons than the regular faculty or staff colleague.

Thus, blue ocean thinking can help differentiate when planning more strategically how to become a successful, transcendental dean. Posner (2009) labels deans as pracademics, perpetuating this Janus-faced role in which hermaphrodite needs to clarify the primary role. Deciding in favour of one or the other in order to become a professional dean simplifies life, careers, resource allocation and self-branding.

The suggestion to establish the career path of professional deans can also signal to business schools and its stakeholders that it is not enough to temporarily promote an individual basically to the level of his or her incompetency as described by the Peter Principle (Ovans, 2014). Proposing to next-generation aspiring candidates to brand themselves authentically as professional deans can help professionalise practices.

This idea of pracademics can be spun further and woven together with the ongoing learning needs. Kegan and Lahey (2009) outline a useful framework that can be applied to dean careers and learning needs if one adopts a more long-term view. As illustrated in figure 10 adapted to business schools, learning in terms of developing mental complexity until a few decades ago foresaw two stages. The formative years of adult learning grew an individual's knowledge and skill set, which then served for the rest of a lifetime. Conceptually, this applied to professors as well, who learned their teaching and research skills and used them later on.

Figure 10 : Application of Kegan and Lahey's (2009) view on a dated understanding of adult brain development to business schools

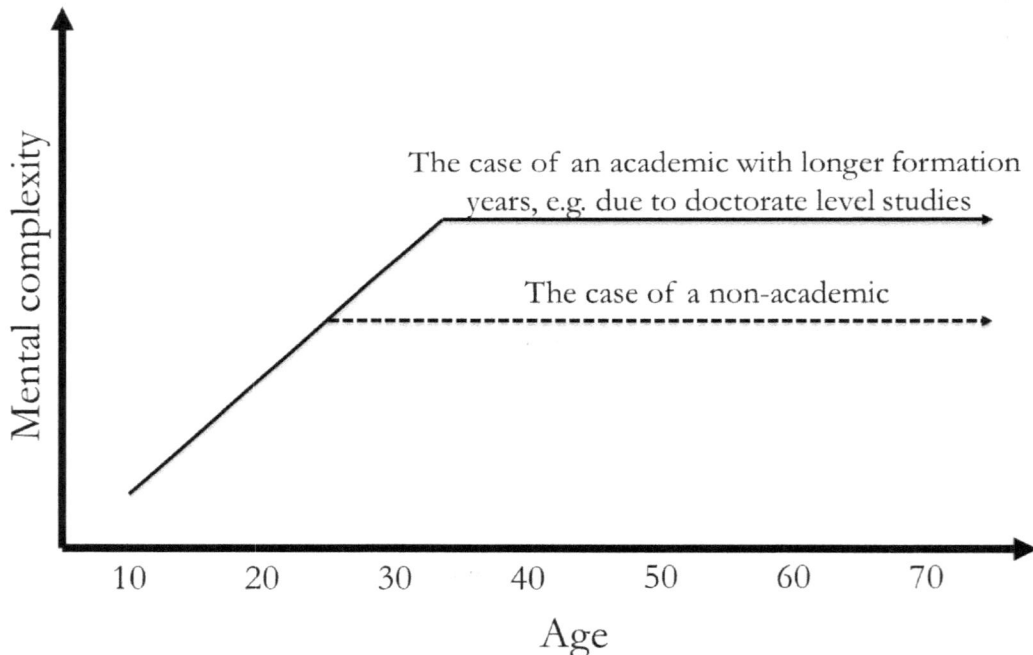

Source: Author, based on Kegan and Laskow Lahey (2009)

The author's more recent research is illustrated in figure 11. It envisages selected individuals' progress to different plateaus of adult brain development over their lifetime. Initially, an individual joining a business school as an academic would develop and have to portray a socialised mind. The selected individuals need to adapt to an organisation's evaluation system, comply with an organisational culture and align themselves with the dominant personalities or logics being taught.

Subsequently, as part of a further learning and maturation process, an individual would progress to the next plateau, evolving a previously rather socialised mind into a self-authoring one. This can lead to the development of a personal agenda, an own compass or reference frame, for example, regarding what constitutes good teaching, research, content, etc. The individual becomes more independent across various dimensions.

Figure 11: Application of Kegan and Lahey's (2009) concept of plateaus of adult brain development to business schools

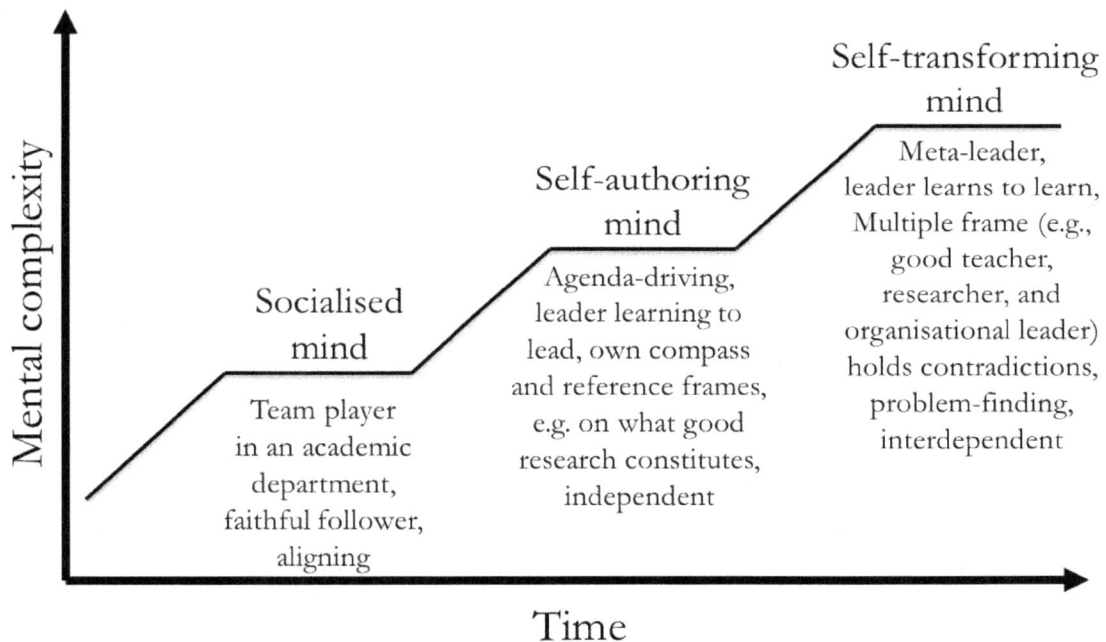

Source: Author, based on Kegan and Lahey (2009)

Eventually, if further learning and development occur, the individual could progress to the next plateau. Here, a self-authoring mind is in place, which can lead across a variety of issues, research, teaching and administrative teams, for example. The individuals on this level hold multiple frames of reference in parallel and can deal with demanding, conflicting and even highly contradictory targets. The candidate for this level seeks and effectively prioritises problems, along with becoming rather interdependent with the surrounding business school context. Individuals on this plateau learn how to learn, very much in line with the accelerated learning journeys and demands identified by the concept of the leadership-oriented ship canal.

What does this boil down to for candidates who aspire to dean positions? They have to understand that in the early career phases the importance of a socialised mind is higher and ensures their membership in the business school community. As a self-authoring mind, they then excel at areas such that they emerge on the radars of those who recruit deans. In order to really excel in the dean assignment, they ought to embrace a self-authoring mind, become fast learners and balance contradicting multiple frames simultaneously. More concretely, they require shifts in strengths, for example, from being a thought leader in research or a star in the classroom with effective teaching routines towards equally effective transformational and transcendental leadership skills.

This train of thought is just as true if one joins a business school from another institution. This logic also applies if a candidate for a dean position originates from the non-academic part of a business school. This occurs more rarely, since academic credentials usually matter as outlined in the aforementioned reference to Tovstiga (2015).

5.6. Summary

This section highlighted the relevant implications for key stakeholder groups both on an institutional as well as an individual level. There is a lot of work to be done when it comes to maturing the available body of knowledge on leadership in general and the specific contexts, for example, the business school context and general versus specific career paths, such as deans. This chapter equally discusses implications for the aspiring next generation leader who might ponder about becoming dean one day. The emerging insight diverges from what Posner (2009) labelled pracademics. Pracademics aim for both practice-orientated and academic credibility. Instead, so-called professional deans make a clear choice and as such can avoid a wrong version of identity crafting as a coping mechanism for a role and identify conflict. Professional deans make a choice to serve as deans, even if this means driving their own development and relinquishing control over an otherwise rather academic career.

6. Conclusions

This study focused on the leadership development of a sample of business school deans. The research question is focused on how this group of leaders in business schools prepare themselves and experience their learning as well as development journey. The initial literature review targeting key sensitising topics already pointed to the role ambiguity along with a lack of research on their development. Addressing this gap, the empirical study explored relevant experiences and produced the framework of a leadership-oriented ship canal. Within the scope and limitations of this study, this framework fits better than the concept of a leadership pipeline proposed in the more general literature on leadership development for the non-academic corporate sector.

The leadership-oriented ship canal posits that leadership development represents learning while doing as well as learning on the job. Long-term development is often lacking. The onboarding period is shortened when contrasted to a leadership pipeline. For the most part, becoming and remaining dean is not even desirable. The role ambiguity renders an active preparation more difficult but does not fully explain the quite clear absence of internal development plans.

Ambiguity remained after discussing the leadership-oriented-ship-canal concept with the help of additional literature in section 4.8. Impression management and crafting identities as a coping mechanism for conflicting roles cannot be fully ruled out. However, the development of the ship canal as a theory grounded in new data gathered with the help of interviews could serve as the foundation for propositions, corresponding hypothesis building and subsequent testing. How to best conceptualise and operationalise these propositions, hypotheses and experiments further, however, falls outside the scope of this study and could form the core of subsequent research. Future studies could inquire into the following: 1) Business schools as organisations have no long-term development plans for deans; 2) early-career professors do not have long-term plans to become dean; 3) the deanship does not represent a desirable, long-term career goal for early-career faculty members; 4) the more an external market for deans is deemed efficient, the less efforts are invested internally to form deans in long-term plans; 5) deans play identity games to pre-empt criticism or to turn criticism into something more positive; and 6) the transcendental leadership orientation dominates amongst business schools. Pursuing these emerging themes further can help generalise beyond the qualitative dataset gathered in the interviews described above. The field of leadership development in this specific context of business schools bears substantially more potential than this preliminary qualitative study could cover.

To conclude, the field of leadership development in business schools gains an initial context-specific framework and presents avenues for further research. In light of the tremendous criticism that business schools face along with the demands and promises brought about by spreading PRME, implications include three major aspects before personal lessons ensue.

When it comes to the field of leadership development in general, leadership pipelines as a concept might not be context-specific enough and represent a more overengineered solution than leadership-oriented ship canals. At times, leadership development must be accelerated.

At the institutional level, business schools gain a framework upon which they can reflect. Business schools are encouraged if their current practices yield the right pool – quantitatively and qualitatively – of talents for future dean roles.

The possibility of ignoring the need to help build the next generation of leaders has risks. When it comes to the next generation of aspiring candidates for the dean position, the conclusion is more reflection as well. If the deans represented in this study can adequately describe their experiences, aspiring to such a role might well have to be reconsidered. It is possible that intentionally choosing to become dean and preparing accordingly can overcome the dilemmas as well. If deans more or less consciously play impression games, then aspiring next-generation deans ought to reflect upon ethics and the extent to which different value behaviours are needed.

On a more personal level and in light of the context of my employer, I learned that the interviewed deans – no other claim to generalisation is made – appear frustrated, disenchanted, unprepared and not showing enough of transformational leadership behaviour. Leadership-oriented ship canals can help explain the phenomenon from a description point of view. It is not a prescriptive model in the first place but there are lessons to be learnt. The limited diverse manners of preparing and each interviewee's narrative about success drivers were enormously revealing. Currently, my employer falls into the category of refrainers in terms of leadership development. This saves cost and may well avoid expectations to recruit one of the next deans from within. In light of ongoing challenges in the marketplace, more leadership skills can foster motivation and organizational readiness to cope with them.

Furthermore, this research project is important for career planning of aspiring individuals. As for the emerging pattern, what is required for the role of dean is an individual with the right identity in mind. A professor without the eagerness to serve as dean, without this servant leadership orientation, may well only serve a shorter and less convincing tenure than an individual who has prepared over years for the dean role and who finds fulfilment and achieves self-actualisation. This research project argues in favour of the rise of such professional deans, which in turn would need to build their formative years on more than the current practices identified in the interviews. More is needed than the rather pragmatic leadership canal.

References

- Agarwal, A. (2018, October 31). Why today's professionals are taking the career road less travelled. Forbes. https://www.forbes.com/sites/anantagarwal/2018/10 /31/why-todays-professionals-are-taking-the-career-road-less-traveled/#6385d 8fa466b

- Allan, G. (2003). A critique of using grounded theory as a research method. *Electronic Journal of Business Research Methods, 2*(1), 1–10. http://www.ejbrm.com/issue/download.html?idIssue=16

- Amann, W. (2014). Fighting the McDonald's phenomenon. In W. Amann, S. Khan, A. Stachowicz-Stanusch, & S. Tripathi (Eds.), *Innovations in executive education* (pp.11–48). Winterwork.

- Amann, W., Pirson, M., Spitzeck, H., Dierksmeier, C., & Von Kimakowitz, E. (Eds.). (2011). *Business schools under fire – humanistic management education as the way forward*. Palgrave.

- Amann, W. (2017). Trends in business school environments and the leadership style of deans. In W. Amann & J. Goh, *Phronesis in business school* (pp. 157–172). IAP.

- Ancona, D., Malone, T., Orlikowski, W., & Senge, P. (2007). In praise of the incomplete leader. *Harvard Business Review, 85*(2), 92–100.

- Anderson, B., & Adams, W. (2016). *Mastering leadership. An integrated framework for breakthrough performance and extraordinary business results*. Wiley.

- Arthur, M., & Rousseau, D. (1996). The boundaryless career as a new employment principle. In M. Arthur & D. Rousseau (Eds.), *The boundaryless career* (pp. 3–20). Oxford University Press.

- Ashby, W. (2011). Variety, constraint, and the law of requisite variety. *Emergence: Complexity & Organization, 13*(1/2), 190–207.

- Athens, L. (1994). The self as a soliloquy. *The Sociological Quarterly, 35*, 521–532.

- Baker, S., & Edwards, R. (2012) How many qualitative interviews is enough. National Centre for Research Methods. http://eprints.ncrm.ac.uk/2273/4/how_many_inter views.pdf

- Beal, J. (2007). Accelerated baccalaureate programs: What we know and what we need to know – Setting a research agenda. Journal of Nursing Education, 46(9), 387–388.

- Bennis, W., & Nanus, B. (1985). *Leaders: The strategies for taking charge.* Harper and Row.

- Bentz, V., & Shapiro, J. (1998). Mindful inquiry in social research. Sage.

- Berger, R. (2015). Now I see it, now I don't: researcher's position and reflexivity in qualitative research. *Qualitative Research, 15*(2), 219–234.

- Breckenridge, J, Jones, D., Elliott, I., & Nicol, M. (2012). Choosing a methodological path: Reflections on the constructivist turn. *Grounded Theory Review, 11*(1), http://groundedtheoryreview.com/2012/06/01/choosing-a-methodological-path-reflections-on-the-constructivist-turn/

- Billot, J. (2010). The imagined and the real: identifying the tensions for academic identity. *Higher Education Research and Development,* 29(6), 709–721.

- Birks, M., Chapman, Y., & Francis, K. (2008). Memoing in qualitative research: Probing data and processes. *Journal of Research in Nursing, 13*(1) 68–75.

- Blaxter, L., Hughes, C., & Tight, M. (2006). How to research (3rd Ed.). Open University Press.

- Boal, K. (2000). Strategic leadership research: Moving on. *Leadership Quarterly, 11*(4), 515–527.

- Bok, D. (2003). *Universities in the marketplace: The commercialization of higher education.* Princeton University Press.

- Bolden, R., Hawkins, B., Gosling, J., & Taylor, S. (2013). *Exploring leadership: individual, organizational, and societal perspectives.* Oxford University Press.

- Bolden, R., Petrov, G., Gosling, J., & Bryman, A. (2009). Leadership in higher education: Facts, fictions and futures. Introduction to the special issue. *Leadership, 5*(3), 291–298.

- Bolman, L., & Deal, T. (1991). *Reframing organizations: Artistry, choice and leadership.* Jossey-Bass.

- Borton, T. (1970). *Reach, teach and touch.* Graw Hill.

- Bowen, G. (2008). Naturalistic inquiry and the saturation concept: A research note. *Qualitative Research, 8*(1), 12–33.

- Boyd, D. (2007). Effective teaching in accelerated learning programs. *Adult Learning,* 15(1/2), 40-43.

- Bradner, D. (1996). *Accelerated learning methodology applied to a corporate training program.* [Unpublished doctoral dissertation]. Iowa State University. https://lib.dr.iastate.edu/rtd/11364

- Brandenburg, U., & Federkeil, G. (2007). *How to measure internationality and internationalization of higher education institutions: Indicators and key figures.* CHE.

- Briscoe, J., & Hall, D. (2006). The interplay of boundaryless and protean careers: Combinations and implications. *Journal of Vocational Behavior, 69,* 4–18.

- Brown, A., Lewis, M., & Oliver, N. (2019). Identity work, loss, and preferred identities: A study of UK business school deans. *Organizations Studies,* June, 1–22.

- Brown, L. (2001). The leadership pipeline – How to build the leadership-powered company. *Business Book Review, 18*(9), 1–10, http://urban-forum.com/articles/Business%20Book%20Review%20-%20The%20Leadership%20Pipeline.pdf

- Bruch, H., & Menges, J. (2010). The acceleration trap. *Harvard Business Review, 88*(4), 80–86.

- Bulmer, M. (1987). Ethics in social research. In J. Kuper (Ed.), *Methods, ethics and models* (pp. 19–22). Routledge & Kegan Paul.

- Burd, E., Smith, S., & Reisman, S. (2015). Exploring business models for MOOCs in higher education. *Innovative Higher Education, 40*(1), 37–50.

- Cameron, E., & Green, M. (2012). *Making sense of change management: A complete guide to the models, tools, and techniques of organizational change.* Kogan.

- Burke, R. (2006). Why leaders fail: Exploring the dark side. *International Journal of Manpower, 27*(1), 91–100.

- Canals, J. (2011). *The future of leadership development.* Palgrave.

- Catino, M. (2014). How do mafias organize? Conflict and violence in three mafia organizations. *European Journal of Sociology, 55*(2), 177–220.

- Cassell, C. (2009). Interviews in organizational research. In D. Buchanan & A. Bryman (Eds.), *The SAGE handbook of organizational research methods,* (pp. 500–515). Sage.

- Chandrasegaran, S., Badam, S., Kisselburgh, L., Peppler, K., Elmqvist, N., & Ramani, K. (2017). VizScribe: A visual analytics approach to understand designer behavior. *International Journal of Human-Computer Studies. 100*(April), 66–80.

- Charan, R., Noel, J., & Drotter, S. J. (2011). The leadership pipeline: how to build the leadership powered company. Jossey-Bass.

- Charmaz, K. (2006). Constructing grounded theory: A practical guide through qualitative analysis. Sage.

- Charmaz, K. (2014). Constructing grounded theory. Sage.

- Charmaz, K. (2000). Grounded theory: Objectivist and constructivist methods. In N. Denzin & Y. Lincoln (Eds.), Handbook of qualitative research (pp. 509–535). Sage.

- Christians, C. (2000). Ethics and politics in qualitative research. In N. Denzin & Y. LincolnF (Eds.), Handbook of qualitative research (pp. 133–154). Sage.

- Chumbley, T (2019). Tom Chumbley on transcendental leadership. https://www.researchgate.net /publication/333728849_Tom_Chumbley_On_Transcendental_Leadership

- Cohen, L., Manion, L., & Morrison, K. (2011). Research methods in education. Routledge.

- Colbert, A., Judge, T., Choi, D., & Wang, G. (2012). Assessing the trait theory of leadership using self and observer ratings of personality: The mediating role of contributions to group success. The Leadership Quarterly, 23(4), 670–685.

- Collis, J., & Hussey, R. (2003). Business research: a practical guide for undergraduate and postgraduate students. Palgrave Macmillan.

- Contractor, F., Kumar, V., & Kundu, S. (2007). Nature of the relationship between international expansion and performance: the case of emerging market firms. Journal of World Business, 42(4), 401–417

- Corbin, J., & Strauss, A. (2012). Basics of Qualitative Research: Techniques and procedures for developing grounded theory. Sage.

- Creswell, J. (2014). Research design: qualitative, quantitative, and mixed methods approaches. Sage.

- D'Alessio, F., & Avolio, B. (2011). Business schools and resources constraints: A task for deans or magicians? *Research in Higher Education Journal, 13,* 1–37. https://pdfs.semanticscholar.org /7c04/84be8965fa82e1f707997adb8358bf6df36c.pdf?_ga=2.262044687.329444916.1570346259 -1514014358.1570346259

- Dameron, S., & Durand, T. (2017). *The future of management education.* Palgrave Macmillan.

- Dann, R., Basford, J., Booth, C., O'Sullivan, R., Scanlon, J., Woodfine, C., & Wright, P.

- (2019). The impact of doctoral study on university lecturers' construction of self within a changing higher education policy context. *Studies in Higher Education, 44*(7), 1166–1182.

- Datar, S., Garvin, D., & Cullen, P. (2010). *Rethinking the MBA: business education at a crossroads.* Harvard Business School Press.

- Davies, J., & Hilton, T. (2014). Building better business schools. *Global Focus, 8*(1), 52–55.

- Davies, J., & Thomas, H. (2010). What do deans do? Insights from a UK study. *Management Decision, 47*(9), 1396–1419.

- Davies, J. (2014). *Hybrid upper middle* manager strategizing practices: Linking archetypes and contingencies in the UK business school deanship. [Unpublished doctorate dissertation]. University of Warwick. http://wrap.warwick.ac.uk/71026/1/WRAP_THESIS_Davies_2014.pdf

- Davies, J. (2016). Are business school deans doomed? The global financial crisis, Brexit and all that. *Journal of Management Development, 35*(7), 901–915.

- Davies, J., & Thomas, H. (2009). What do business school deans do? Insights from a UK study. *Management Decision, 47*(9), 1396–1419.

- Dawson, S. (2008). Building a business school at the heart of Cambridge. In Aspatore Books (Ed.), *Business school management. Top educational leaders on creating a strong school reputation, offering competitive programs, and thriving in the educational marketplace* (pp. 157–174). Thomson.

- De Geus, A. (1988). Planning as learning. Harvard Business Review, March. Retrieved from https://hbr.org/1988/03/planning-as-learning

- Denzin, N. (1970). *The research act. A theoretical introduction to sociological methods.* McGraw-Hill.

- Denzin, N., & Lincoln, Y. (2000). Handbook of qualitative research. Sage.

- Dew, K. (2014). *Structural functionalism.* Wiley.

- Dey, I. (1999). *Grounding grounded theory.* Academic Press.

- DiMarco, N., Kuehl, C., & Wims, E. (1975). Leadership style and interpersonal need orientation as moderators of changes in leadership dimension scores. *Personnel Psychology, 28*, 210–218.

- Dixon, L. (2016, November 30). How long should a CEO's tenure be? Talent Economy. https://www.chieflearningofficer.com/2016/11/30/long-ceos-tenure/

- Eisenhardt, K (1989), Building theories from case study research. *Academy of Management Review*, *14*(4), 532–550.

- Eisenhardt, K, & Graebner, M. (2007). Theory building from cases: Opportunities and challenges. *The Academy of Management Journal*, *50*(1), 25–32.

- Engwall, L. (2007). The anatomy of management education. *Scandinavian Journal of Management*, 23(1), 4–35.

- Estermann, T., Pruvot, E., & Claeys-Kulik, A.-L (2013). Designing strategies for efficient funding of higher education in Europe - Interim report. http://www.eua.be/activities-services /projects/past-projects/governance-autonomy-and-funding/designing-strategies-for-efficient-funding-of-higher-education-in-europe-(define)

- Evans, G., & Liverpool, J. (2013). A novice researcher's first walk through the maze of grounded theory: Rationalization for classical grounded theory. Grounded Theory Review: An International Journal, 12(1). http://groundedtheoryreview .com

- Fernandez, C. (2012). Guest editorial. *The Grounded Theory Review*, *11*(1), 7–28.

- Fink, A. (2005). *Conducting research literature reviews: From the Internet to paper*. Sage Publications.

- Fischer, C. (2008). Bracketing in qualitative research: Conceptual and practical matters. *Psychotherapy Research*, *19*(4-5), 583–590.

- Fisher, A., & Tallant, J. (2015). Can teaching philosophy in schools count towards the Research Excellence Framework (UK)? Cogent Education, 2(1). https://doaj.org/article /6aeb0a60daa449d79725996ee490191d

- Fleenor, J., & Van Velsor, E. (1993). The relationship between benchmarks and personality measures used in the leadership development program. Center for Creative Leadership.

- Ford, K. (2010). Reframing a sense of self: a constructivist grounded theory study of children's admission to hospital for surgery. PhD thesis, University of Tasmania. https://eprints.utas.edu.au /10771/

- Forray, J., Leigh, J., & Kenworthy, A. L. (2015). Special section cluster on responsible management education: Nurturing an emerging PRME ethos. *Academy of Management Learning & Education, 14*(2), 293–296.

- Fragueiro, F., & Thomas, H. (2010). Keeping one step ahead. *Global Focus, 4*(3), 14–17.

- Furnham, A. (2008). Psychometric correlates of FIRO-B scores: Locating the FIRO-B scores in personality factor space. *International Journal of Selection and Assessment, 16*(1), 30–45.

- Gardner, J. (1990). *On leadership.* The Free Press.

- Garic, D. (2006). Are leaders born or made? *Supervision, 67*(12), 19–20.

- Ghemawat, P. (2007). Managing differences: The central challenge of global strategy. *Harvard Business Review, 85*(3), 58–68.

- Ghemawat, P. (2011). *World 3.0: Global prosperity and how to achieve it.* Harvard Business Review Press.

- Glaser, B. (1978). *Theoretical sensitivity.* The Sociology Press.

- Glaser, B. (1992). *Basics of grounded theory analysis.* The Sociology Press

- Glaser, B. (2001). *The grounded theory perspective: Conceptualization contrasted with description.* The Sociology Press.

- Glaser, B. (2002). Constructivist grounded theory? *Forum: Qualitative Social Research, 3*(3). http://nbn-resolving.de/urn:nbn:de:0114-fqs0203125.

- Glaser, B. (2007). Constructivist grounded theory? *Historical Social Research, Supplement, 19,* 93–105.

- Glaser, B. G. (2012). Constructivist grounded theory? *Grounded Theory Review:* An International Journal, 11(1). http://groundedtheoryreview.com/2012/06/01/constructivist-grounded-theory/

- Glaser, B. (2013). Introduction: Free style memoing. Grounded Theory Review – An International Journal, 2(4), http://groundedtheoryreview.com/2013/12/22/introduction-free-style-memoing/

- Glaser, B., & Strauss, A. (1967). *The discovery of grounded theory.* Aldine.

- Gmelch, W., Wolverton, M., Wolverton, M., & Sarros, J. (1999). The academic dean: An imperilled species searching for balance. *Research in Higher Education, 40*(6), 717–740.

- Godemann, J., Haertle, J., Herzig, C., & Moon, J. (2014). United Nations supported principles for responsible management education: Purpose, progress and prospects. *Journal of Cleaner Production, 62*(16), 16–23.

- Goethals, G., & Sorenson, G. (2006). *The quest for a general theory of leadership*. Edward Elgar.

- Goffman, E. (1958). *The presentation of self in everyday life*. University of Edinburgh.

- Goffman, E. (1963). *Stigma: Notes on the management of spoiled identity*. Prentice Hall.

- Goleman, D. (2000). Leadership that gets results. *Harvard Business Review, 78*(2), 78–90.

- Goldsmith, M., & Reiter, M. (2007). *What got you here won't get you there*. Hyperion.

- Grau, D. (2019). Self-leadership and interpersonal competences of future aspiring professionals in the Arab Middle East: Reference to FIRO-B. *Management Science Letters, 9*, 2021–2028.

- Greenhaus, J., Callanan, G., & DiRenzo, M. (2008). A boundaryless perspective on careers. In J. Barling (Ed.), *Handbook of organizational behavior* (pp. 277–299). Sage.

- Greenleaf, R. (1970). *The servant as a leader*. The Greenleaf Center.

- Gregory, R., Beck, R., Keil, M. (2013). Control balancing in information systems development offshoring projects. *Management Information Systems Quarterly, 37*(4), 1211–1232.

- Gregory, R., Keil, M., Muntermann, J., & Mähring, M. (2015). Paradoxes and the nature of ambidexterity in IT transformation programs. *Information Systems Research, 26*(1), 57–80.

- Hall, D. (1996). Protean careers of the 21st century. *Academy of Management Executive, 10*(4), 8–16.

- Harzing, A.-W. (2010). An empirical analysis and extension of the Bartlett and Ghoshal typology of multinational companies. *Journal of International Business Studies, 31*(1), 101–120.

- Hassan, A. (2013). *Leadership styles of business school deans and their perceived effectiveness*. [Unpublished doctoral thesis]. Brunel University. http://bura.brunel.ac.uk/handle/2438/9121

- Heizmann, S. (2003). "Because of you I am an invalid!" - Some methodological reflections about the limitations of collecting and interpreting verbal data and the attempt to win new insights by applying the epistemological potential of ethnopsychoanalytical concepts. Forum: Qualitative Social Research, 4(2). http://nbn-resolving.de/urn:nbn:de:0114-fqs0302315

- Hennink, M., Kaiser, B., & Marconi, V. (2017). Code saturation versus meaning saturation: How many interviews are enough? *Qualitative Health Research*, *27*(4), 591–608.

- Henslin, J., Possamai, A., Possamai-Inesedy, A., Marjoribanks, T., & Elder, K. (2015). *Sociology: A down to earth approach*. Pearson.

- Heron, J., & Reason, P. (1997). A participatory inquiry paradigm. *Qualitative Inquiry, 3*(3), 274–294.

- Hiller, N., DeChurch, L., Murase, T., & Doty, D. (2011). Searching for outcomes of leadership: A 25-year review. *Journal of Management*, *37*(4), 1137–1177.

- Hoare, K., Mills, J., & Francis, K. (2012). Dancing with data: an example of acquiring theoretical sensitivity in a grounded theory study. *International Journal of Nursing Practice*, *18*(3), 240–245.

- Hodgson, P., & White, R. (2001). *Relax, it is only uncertainty*. Prentice Hall.

- Hogan, J., Hogan, R., & Kaiser, R. (2010). Management derailment: Personality assessment and mitigation. In S. Zedeck (Ed.), American Psychological Association handbook of industrial and organizational psychology (pp. 555–575). American Psychological Association.

- Holstein, J. A., & Gubrium, J. F. (2004). The active interview. In D. Silverman (Ed.), *Qualitative research: Theory, method, and practice* (pp. 140–161). Sage.

- Huber, G., & Power, D. (1985). Retrospective reports of strategic-level managers: Guidelines for increasing their accuracy. *Strategic Management Journal*, *6*(2), 171–180.

- Hurley, J. (1989). Dubious support for FIRO-B validity. *Psychological Reports, 65*, 929–930.

- Imel, S. (2002). Accelerated learning in adult education and training and development. *Trends and Issues Alert*, 33. https://eric.ed.gov/?id=ED462551

- Ingraham, P., & Getha-Taylor, H. (2004). Leadership in the public sector. Review of Public Personnel Administration, 24(2), 95-112.

- Iñiguez de Onzoño, S. (2011). *The learning curve*. Palgrave Macmillan.

- Iñiguez de Onzoño, S., & Carmona, S. (2012). A red queen approach to the fading margins of business education. *Journal of Management Development*, *31*(4), 386–397.

- Ivory, C., Misekll, P., Shipton, H., White A., & Moeslein, K. (2006). The future of UK business schools. AIM research. http://wi1.uni-erlangen.de/files/busschool.pdf

- Jago, A. (1982). Leadership: Perspectives in theory and research. *Management Science, 28*(3), 315–336.

- Jao, J. (2014, November 13). Why CEOs need mentors – They accelerate learning. *Management Lessons* Leadership. https://www.entrepreneur.com/article/239682

- Kabele, J. (2010). The agency/structure dilemma: A coordination solution. *Journal for the Theory of Social Behaviour, 40*(3), 314–338.

- Kaiser, R. (2011). The leadership pipeline: Fad, fashion, or empirical fact? An introduction to the special issue. *The Psychologist-Manager Journal, 14*(2), 71–75.

- Kaplan, R., & Kaiser, R.B. (2003). Developing versatile leadership. *MIT Sloan Management Review, 44*(4), 19–26.

- Kegan, R., & Laskow Lahey, L. (2009). *Immunity to change: How to overcome it and unlock potential in yourself and your organization.* Harvard Business School Press.

- Kellerman, B. (2012). *The end of leadership.* Harper Collins.

- Ketokivi, M., Mantere, S., & Cornelissen, J. (2017). Reasoning by analogy and the progress of theory. *Academy of Management Review, 42*(4), 637–658.

- Kezar, A., & Holcombe, E. (2017). *Shared leadership in higher education: Important lessons from research and practice.* American Council on Education. https://www.acenet.edu/Documents/Shared-Leadership-in-Higher-Education.pdf

- Khan, H. (2011). A literature review of corporate governance International Conference on E-business, Management and Economics. IPEDR Vol.25. http://www.ipedr.com/vol25/1-ICEME2011-A10015.pdf

- Khurana, R. (2004). *Searching for a corporate savior: The irrational quest for charismatic CEOs.* Princeton University Press.

- Killi, S., & Morrison, A. (2015). Just-in-time teaching, just-in-need learning: Designing towards optimized pedagogical outcomes. *Universal Journal of Educational Research, 3*(10), 742–750.

- Kilner, A. (2015). Manager or specialist. Which role is most suitable for you? *Holistic Marketing Management, 5*(1), 6–10.

- Kim, W., & Mauborgne, R. (2014). Blue ocean leadership: are your employees fully engaged in moving your company forward? Here's how to release their untapped talent and energy. *Harvard Business Review*, *5*, 60–72.

- Kirkpatrick, D. (1976). Evaluation of training. In R. Craig (Ed.), *Training and development handbook: A guide to human resource development* (pp. 317–319). McGraw Hill.

- Klein, G., Koller, T., & Lovallo, D. (2019). Bias busters: Premortems: Being smart at the start. *McKinsey Quarterly*, April. https://www.mckinsey.com/business-functions/strategy-and-corporate-finance/our-insights/bias-busters-premortems-being-smart-at-the-start

- Knowles, M., Holton, E., & Swanson, R. (2011). *The adult learner – The definitive classic in adult education and human resource development*. Butterworth-Heinemann.

- Kompanje, E. J. O. (2018). Burnout, boreout and compassion fatigue on the ICU: it is not about work stress, but about lack of existential significance and professional performance. Intensive Care Medicine, 44(5). https://www.researchgate.net/publication/323313538_Burnout_boreout_and_compassion_fatigue_on_the_ICU_it_is_not_about_work_stress_but_about_lack_of_existential_significance_and_professional_performance

- Kovaks, G. (2012). The role of the dean. In W. Amann, P. Fenton, P. Zackariasson, & M. Kerrets (Eds.), *New perspectives on management education* (pp. 86–101). Excel Publishing.

- Krause, N., Anderson, M., & Thompson, R. (2008). *Validation of the FIRO-B instrument with benchmarks performance dimensions*. CPP.

- Kring, K., & Kaplan, S. (2011). *The business school dean* redefined. The Korn/Ferry Institute. http://static.kornferry.com/media/sidebar_downloads/The%20business%20school%20dean%20redefined-%20New%20leadership%20requirements%20from%20the%20front%20lines%20of%20change%20in%20academia.pdf

- Lai, C. Y., Lange, A., List, J. A., & Price, M. K. (2017). The business of business is business: Why (some) firms should provide public goods when they sell private goods. [NBER Working Paper No. 23105]. National Bureau of Economic Research. https://www.nber.org/papers/w23105

- Langley, A., & Meziani, N. (2020). Making interviews meaningful. *The Journal of Applied Behavioral Science*, 56(3), 370–391.

- Lassig, J. (2012) Perceiving and pursuing novelty: a grounded theory of adolescent creativity. PhD thesis, Queensland University of Technology. https://eprints.qut.edu.au/50661/

- Lesha, J. (2014). Action research in education. *European Scientific Journal*, *10*(13), 379–386.

- Lincoln, Y., Lynham, S., & Guba, E. (2011). Paradigmatic controversies, contradictions, and emerging confluences, revisited. In N. Denzin & Y. Lincoln (Eds.), The Sage handbook of qualitative research, pp. 97–128). Sage.

- Lombardo, M., & Eichinger, R. (2000). High potentials as high learners. *Human Resource Management*, *39*(4), 321–329.

- Lorange, P. (2002). *New vision for management education: leadership challenges*. Pergamon.

- Lorange, P. (2008). *Thought leadership meets business*. Cambridge University Press.

- Luebbecke, E., Luebbecke, M., & Moehring, R. (2014). Ship traffic optimization for the Kiel canal. https://www.researchgate.net/publication/268982408_Ship_Traffic_Optimization_for_the_Kiel_Canal

- Maclean, M., Harvey, C., & Chia, R. (2012). Sensemaking, storytelling and the legitimization of elite business careers. Human Relations, 65(1), 17–40.

- MacLeod, L. (2012). Making SMART goals smarter. *Physician Executive*, *38*(2), 68–70.

- Macrosson, W., & Semple, J. (2016). FIRO-B, Machiavellianism, and teams. *Psychological Report*, *88*(3), 1187–1193.

- Mahler, W., & Wrightnour, W. (1973). *Executive continuity: How to build and retain an effective management team*. Dow Jones-Irwin.

- Mainiero, L., & Sullivan, S. (2005). Kaleidoscope careers: An alternative explanation for the "opt-out generation". *Academy of Management Executive*, *19*, 106–123.

- Marzano, R., & Kendall, J. (2007). *The new taxonomy of educational objectives*. Corwin Press.

- Mason, M. (2010). Sample size and saturation in PhD studies using qualitative interviews. Forum: Qualitative Social Research, 11(3). http://www.qualitative-research.net/index.php/fqs/article/view/1428/3027

- Maxwell, J. (2011). *The 5 levels of leadership: Proven steps to maximize your potential*. Hachette Book Group.

- McCauley, C. (2020). Making leadership happen. Center for Creative leadership. https://cclinnovation.org/wp-content/uploads/2020/02/making-leadership-happen.pdf

- McGhee, G., Marland G., & Atkinson J. (2007). Grounded theory research: Literature reviewing and reflexivity. *Journal of Advanced Nursing, 60*(3), 334–342.

- Mehta, S. (2011). The culture of corporate social responsibility (CSR) in the academic framework: Some literary implications. *Contemporary Issues in Education Research, 4*(10), 19–24.

- Miller, S., & Fredericks, M. (1999). How does grounded theory explain? *Qualitative Inquiry, 9*, 538–551.

- Millo, Y., & Schinckus, C. (2016). A nuanced perspective on episteme and techne in finance. *International Review of Financial Analysis, 46*, 124–130.

- Mills, J., Clayton, V., Bonner, A., & Francis, K. (2008). The development of constructivist grounded theory. *International Journal of Qualitative Methods, 5*(1), 25–35.

- Mills, J.; Bonner, A., & Francis, K. (2006). Adopting a constructivist approach to grounded theory: Implications for research design. *International Journal of Nursing Practice, 12*(1), 8-13.

- Moon, S., Birchall, D., Williams, S., & Charalambos, V. (2005). Developing design principles for an E-Learning programme for SME managers to support accelerated learning at the workplace. *Journal of Workplace Learning, 17*(5/6), 370–384.

- Morse, J. (2000). Determining sample size. *Qualitative Health Research*, 10, 3–5.

- Morse, J. (2011). Molding qualitative health research. *Qualitative Health Research, 21*(8), 1019–21.

- Moses, J., & Knutsen, T. (2012). *Ways of knowing: Competing methodologies in social and political research.* Palgrave Macmillan.

- Mruck, K. & Mey, G. (2007). Grounded theory and reflexivity. In Antony Bryant & Kathy Charmaz (Eds.), The Sage handbook of grounded theory (pp.515-538). Sage.

- Oliver, N., Brown, A., & Lewis, M. (2020). Business school deans: Leadership in a complex, multi-stakeholder environment. https://charteredabs.org/business-school-deans-leadership-complex-multi-stakeholder-environment/

- Nagel, D., Burns, V., Tilley, C., & Aubin, D. (2015). When novice researchers adopt constructivist grounded theory: Navigating less travelled paradigmatic and methodological paths in PhD dissertation work. *International Journal of Doctoral Studies, 10*, 365–383.

- Nikitina, T., & Lapina, I. (2017). Overview of trends and developments in business education. In *Proceedings of* the 21st World Multi-Conference on Systemics, Cybernetics and Informatics (WMSCI 2017) (Vol. 2). http://www.iiis.org/CDs2017/CD2017Summer/

- Opdenakker, R. (2006). Advantages and disadvantages of four interview techniques in qualitative research. *Forum Qualitative Sozialforschung/Forum: Qualitative Social Research, 7*(4), 34–41.

- O'Reilly, C., & Tushman, M. (2004). The ambidextrous organization. *Harvard Business Review, 82*(45), 74–81.

- Ovans, A. (2014, December 22). Overcoming the Peter Principle. Harvard Business Review. https://hbr.org/2014/12/overcoming-the-peter-principle

- Owen, D., & Davidson, J. (2009). Hubris syndrome: An acquired personality disorder? A study of US Presidents and UK Prime Ministers over the last 100 years. *Brain, 132*(5), 1396–1406.

- Palmer, R. (1969). *Hermeneutics: Interpretation theory in Schleiermacher, Dilthey, Heidegger, and Gadamer.* Northwestern University Press.

- Parry, K. (2003). How? And why?: Theory emergence and using grounded theory to determine levels of analysis. In F. Dansereau & F. Yammarino (Eds.), *Multi-Level Issues in Organizational Behavior and Strategy* (pp. 127–141). Emerald.

- Peiperl, M., & Baruch, Y. (1997). Back to square zero: The post-corporate career. *Organizational Dynamics, 25*(4), 7–22.

- Pfeffer, J. (2009). *Leadership Development in Business Schools: An Agenda for Change.* [Working papers]. Stanford Graduate School of Business.

- Philips, J. (1996). Measuring ROI: The fifth level of evaluation. *Technical & Skills Training, April,* 10–13.

- Piaw, C., & Ting, L. (2014). Are school leaders born or made? Examining factors of leadership styles of Malaysian school leaders. *Procedia – Social and Behavioral Sciences, 116,* 5120–5124.

- Pietersen, W. (2015). What Nelson Mandela taught the world about leadership. *Leader to Leader, 76,* 60–66.

- Pirson, M. (2019). A humanistic perspective for management theory: Protecting dignity and promoting well-being. *Journal of Business Ethics, 159*(1), 39–57.

- Posner, P. (2009). The pracademic: An agenda for re-engaging practitioners and academics. *Public Budgeting & Finance, 29*, 12–26.

- Ralph, N., Birks, M., & Chapman, Y. (2015). The methodological dynamism of grounded theory. *International Journal of Qualitative Methods, 14*(4), https://journals.sagepub.com/doi/full/10.1177/1609406915611576

- Reams, J. (2016). Going mainstream: A review of mastering leadership. Integral Review, 12(1), https://integral-review.org/issues/vol_12_no_1_reams_review_of_mastering_leadership.pdf

- Riessman, C. (2008). *Narrative methods for the human sciences*. Sage.

- Riessman, C. (2009). Considering grounded theory: Categories, cases, and control. Review of the book Constructing grounded theory: A practical guide through qualitative analysis. *Symbolic Interaction, 32*, 390–393.

- Rooke, D., & Torbert, W. (2005). Seven transformations of leadership. *Harvard Business Review, 83*(4), 66–76.

- Rosch, D., & Collins, J. (2017). The significance of student organizations to leadership development. *New Directions for Student Leadership, 2017*(155). https://onlinelibrary.wiley.com/doi/abs/10.1002/yd.20246

- Rost, J. (1991). *Leadership for the twenty-first century*. Praeger Publishers.

- Rothstein, B. (2013). Corruption and social trust: Why the fish rots from the head down. *Social Research, 80* (4), 1009–1032.

- Rousseau, D., Manning, J., & Denyer, D. (2008, December 2). Evidence in management and organizational science: Assembling the field's full weight of scientific knowledge through syntheses. SSRN eLibrary. http://papers.ssrn. com/sol3/papers.cfm?abstract_id=1309606

- Salminen, S. (1988). Two psychometric problems of the FIRO-B Questionnaire. Psychological Reports, 63, 423–426.

- Sbaraini, A., Carter, S., Evans, R., & Blinkhorn, A. (2011). How to do a grounded theory study: a worked example of a study of dental practices. BMC Medical Research Methodology, 11, https://bmcmedresmethodol.biomedcentral.com/articles/10.1186/1471-2288-11-128#citeas

- Schornack, G. R. (1996, November). Accelerated learning techniques for adults – An instructional design concept for the next decade. [Paper]. *Fourth Annual College of Career Education Faculty* Symposium on Teaching Effectiveness. https://commons.erau.edu/cgi/viewcontent.cgi?article=1045&context=bollinger-rosado

- Schutz, W. (1958). FIRO: A three-dimensional theory of interpersonal behaviour. Holt, Rinehart-Winston.

- Schutz, W. (1978). *FIRO Awareness scales manual.* Consulting Psychologists Press.

- Schwertfeger, B. (2019a, August 13). Ex-EBS-Präsident Jahns: Neues Hauptverfahren wegen Untreue. MBA Journal online. https://www.mba-journal.de/ex-ebs-praesident-jahns-neues-hauptverfahren-wegen-untreue/

- Schwertfeger, B. (2019b, September 23). EBS: Erneut weniger Studenten. MBA Journal online. https://www.mba-journal.de/ebs-erneut-weniger-studenten/

- Seybolt, J. (1996). Commentary: The case against practicality and relevance as gauges of business schools. *Journal of Management Inquiry, 5*(4), 355–358.

- Shumate, M., & Fulk, J. (2004). Boundaries and role conflict when work and family are collocated: A communication network and symbolic interaction approach. *Human Relations, 57*, 55–74.

- Siggelkow, N. (2007). Persuasion with case studies. *Academy of Management Journal, 50*(1), 20–24.

- Simon, H. (1991). *Models of my life.* Basic Books.

- Singer, A. (2014, October 20). *The four stages of leadership development.* Hartford Business. http://m.hartfordbusiness.com/article/20141020/PRINTEDITION/310179962/the-four-stages-of-leadership-development

- Singh, S., & Estefan, A. (2018). Selecting a grounded theory approach for nursing research. *Global Qualitative Nursing Research, 5*, 1–9.

- Smeyers, P., De Ruyter, D. J., Waghid, Y., & Strand, T. (2014). Publish yet perish: On the pitfalls of philosophy of education in an age of impact factors. *Studies in Philosophy and Education, 33*(6), 647–666.

- Solitander, N., Fougere, M., Sobczak, A., & Herlin, H. (2012). We are the Champions: Organizational learning and change for responsible management education. *Journal of Management Education, 36*(3), 337–363.

- Spender, J., & Locke, R. (2011). *Confronting managerialism: How the business elite and their schools threw our lives out of balance.* Zed Books.

- Starks, H., & Trinidad, S. (2007). Choose your method: A comparison of phenomenology, discourse analysis, and grounded theory. *Qualitative Health Research, 17*(10), 1372–1380.

- Stern, P. (2007). On solid ground: Essential properties of growing grounded theory. In A. Bryant & K. Charmaz (Eds.), *Handbook of grounded theory* (pp. 114–126). Sage.

- Storey, M., Killian, S., & O'Regan, P. (2017). All Responsible management education: Mapping the field in the context of the SDGs. *International Journal of Management Education, 15*(2), 93–103.

- Strauss, A., & Corbin, J. (1990). *Basics of qualitative research: grounded theory procedures and techniques.* Sage.

- Strauss, A., & Corbin, J. (1998). *Basics of qualitative research: Techniques and procedures for developing grounded theory.* Sage.

- Sull, D., & Sull, C. (2018, June 5). With goals, FAST beats SMART. MIT Sloan Management Review. https://sloanreview.mit.edu/article/with-goals-fast-beats-smart/

- Sullivan, S., & Baruch, Y. (2009). Advances in career theory and research: A critical review and agenda for future exploration. Journal of Management, 35(6), 1542–1571.

- Super, D. (1957). Psychology of careers. Harper & Brothers.

- Swanson, D., & Frederick, W. (2011). Are business schools silent partners in corporate crime? The Journal of Corporate Citizenship, 9(1), 24–27.

- Tamunomiebi, M., Omosioni, I., & Odunayo, A. (2018). Church leadership and congregational growth: A review of literature. British Journal of Humanities and Social Sciences, 21(2), 48–58.

- Thomas, G., & James, D. (2006) Reinventing grounded theory: Some questions about theory, ground and discovery. British Educational Research Journal, 32(6), 767–795.

- Thomas, H., & Cornuel, E. (2012). Business schools in transition? Issues of impact, legitimacy, capabilities and re-invention. Journal of Management Development, 31(4), 329–335.

- Thomson, S. (2011). Sample size and grounded theory. Journal of Administration & Governance, 5(1), 1–8. http://www.joaag.com/uploads/5_1__Research_Note_1_Thomson.pdf

- Tie, Y., Birks, M., & Francis, K. (2019, January 2). Grounded theory research: A design framework for novice researchers. SAGE Open Medicine, 7. https://www.ncbi.nlm.nih.gov/pmc/articles/PMC6318722/#bibr27-20503121188 22927

- Thorne, S., & Darbyshire, P. (2005). Land mines in the field: A modest proposal for improving the craft of qualitative health research. Qualitative Health Research, 15(8), 1105–1113.

- Torres, L. E., Ruiz, C. E., Hamlin, B., & Velez-Calle, A. (2015). Perceived managerial and leadership effectiveness in Colombia. European Journal of Training and Development, 39(3), 203–219.

- Tourish, D. (2020). The triumph of nonsense in management studies. Academy of Management Learning & Education, 19(1), https://doi.org/10.5465/aml e.2019.0255

- Tovstiga, G. (2015). *Strategy in practice*. Wiley.

- Tucker, A., & Bryan, R. (1991). *The academic dean: Dove, dragon, and diplomat*. Macmillan.

- Uslu, O. (2019). General overview to leadership theories from a critical perspective. *Marketing and Management of Innovations*, *1*, 161–172. http://doi.org/10.21272/ mmi.2019.1-13

- Van Eeden, R., Cilliers, F., & Van Deventer, V. (2008). Leadership styles and associated personality traits : support for the conceptualisation of transactional and transformational leadership. *South African Journal of Psychology*, *38*(2), 253–267.

- Van Cleeve, M. (1981). *Deaning: Middle management in academe*. University of Illinois Press.

- Van Leeuwen, T. (2001). What is authenticity? *Discourse Studies*, 3(4), 392–397. https://www.jstor.org/stable/24047523?seq=1

- Van Maanen, J. (1979) The fact of fiction in organizational ethnography. *Administrative Science Quarterly*, *24*(4), 539–611.

- Van Maanen, J. (1991). Playing back the tape: Early days in the field. In W. Shaffir and R. Stebbins (eds), *Experiencing fieldwork* (pp. 79-95). Sage.

- Vaught, B., Pettit, J., & Taylor, R. (1989). Interpersonal communication behaviour of male and female administrators. *International Journal of Educational Management*, *3*(2), 14–19.

- Waring, T., & Wainwright, D. (2008). Issues and challenges in the use of template analysis: Two comparative case studies from the field. *Electronic Journal of Business Research Methods, 6*(1), 85–93.

- Watkins, M. (2009). *Your next move: The leader's guide to navigating major career transitions.* Harvard Business Review Press.

- Western, S. (2013). *Leadership: A critical text.* Sage.

- Wihlborg, M., & Robson, S. (2019). Critical viewpoints on the Bologna Process in Europe: Can we do otherwise? *European Educational Research Journal, 18*(2), 135–157.

- Williams, K. (2009). 'Guilty knowledge': Ethical aporia emergent in the research practice of educational development practitioners. London Review of Education, 7(3), 211–221.

- Wohlin, C. (2014). Guidelines for snowballing in systematic literature studies and a replication in software engineering. In *Proceedings of the 18th International Conference on Evaluation and Assessment in Software Engineering.* Association for Computing Machinery.

- Wlodkowski, R. (2003). Accelerated learning in colleges and universities. In R. J. Wlodkowski & C. E. Kasworm (Eds.), *Accelerated learning for adults: The promise and practice of intensive educational formats. New Directions for Adult and Continuing Education* 97 (pp. 5–15). Wiley Periodicals.

- Wright, L., & Leahey, M. (1984). *Nurses and families: A guide to family assessment and intervention.* Davis.

- Wuest, J. (1995). Feminist grounded theory: An exploration of the congruency and tensions between two traditions in knowledge discovery. *Qualitative Health Research, 5*(1), 125–137.

- Zakaria, R., Hatib bin Musta'amal, A. (2014). Building rapport in qualitative research. http://eprints.utm.my/id/eprint/61304/1/AedeHatibMustaamal2014_RapportBuildinginQualitativeResearch.pdf

- Zafirov, M. (2017). The Qatar crisis – Why the blockade failed. *Israel Journal of Foreign Affairs, 11*(2), 191–201.

- Zenger, J., & Folkman, J. (2014). *How extraordinary leaders double profits.* Zenger Folkman.

About the author

Professor Dr. oec. D.Ed.Psy EdD D. Litt. (hon.) Wolfgang Amann graduated from the University of St.Gallen in Switzerland with a doctorate in international strategy. He subsequently added studies in the field of education and learning psychology. He is also a graduate of key faculty development programs, such as Harvard University's Institute for Management and Leadership in Education, IESE's IFP, IMD's ITP, the EFMD International Deans Program, and CEEMAN's IMTA. Besides being active in top management consulting, he has been designing and delivering executive education seminars and advising senior leaders for more than 20 years. He has published 50+ books for executives and compiled 100+ case studies for his executive education seminars. He was previously the executive academic director of the Goethe Business School, dean of the Complexity Management, director of the MBA program family at the University of St.Gallen, and director of the university foundation project of the EBS University, its law school, and supply chain school. He currently serves as professor of strategy and leadership as well as academic director of degree, open enrolment, and custom programs of HEC Paris. He was previously a consultant for and trained executives, for example, at Allianz, Andersen, Bertelsmann, BHF Bank, China Development Bank, Commercial Bank of Qatar, Coke, Daimler, Deutsche Bahn, Deutsche Bank, Deutsche Telekom, Dixon/ DSG, Dupont, Etisalat, European Venture Capital and Private Equity Association, Etisalat, Evonik, Festo, Ford, Generali, Hilti, JPC, Malteser, Msheireb, IBM, IFC/Worldbank, Ikea, Marsoft, Mitsubishi, UN Global Compact/PRME, Office Depot, Proctor&Gamble, Sanofi-Aventis, Tetra Pak, Unicef, W. L. Gore, as well as several UHNW individuals and family offices. He served and serves on several boards and has successfully built up several firms. He frequently delivers keynote speeches at international conferences and has been a guest professor at Hosei University in Tokyo, Japan, Tsinghua in Beijing, and CEIBS in Shanghai, China, the Indian Institute of Management in Bangalore, India, ISP St. Petersburg in Russia, Corvinus University in Hungary, Mzumbe University in Tanzania, Warwick and Henley Business School in the UK, as well as Wharton in the US. He received several research, teaching, and impact awards along with honorary professorships. For example, he won five CEMS Best Course Awards and during his direction of the academic programs at HEC Paris in Qatar, the school won the Enterprise Agility Award & Entrepreneur of the Year 2015, as well as the Educational Institute of the Year Award 2016 from Entrepreneurs Magazine (Middle East).

www.ingramcontent.com/pod-product-compliance
Lightning Source LLC
Chambersburg PA
CBHW081402270326
41930CB00015B/3385